The Spice of Life

The Spice of Life
Cookbook

A World of Healthy & Zesty
Chicken Recipes

Jeffrey C. Leeds

Momentum Books, Ltd.
Troy, Michigan

This book is an independent work. Neither UCLA nor the UCLA Heart Transplant unit nor any of its employees, students, or agents wrote, tested, or created any part of this work.

Author photo by M. David Leeds

Leeds, Jeffrey C., 1944–
    The spice of life : a world of healthy and zesty chicken recipes / ny Jeffrey C. Leeds.
        p.   cm.
    Includes index.
    ISBN 1-879094-60-6 (alk. paper)
    1. Heart--Diseases--Diet therapy. 2. Cookery (Chicken) 3. Low-fat diet--Recipes. 4. Salt-free diet--Recipes. I. Title.
RC684.D5L44 1999
614.5'6311--dc21   99-19169

To the memory of my heart donor…
and to the caring and always life-affirming
people at the UCLA Heart Transplant unit

Acknowledgments

The sincerest thank you to the following people who,
in their own way, and with their own special gifts,
made the realization of this book possible

Dr. Jon Kobashigawa

Johanna Salamandra

Dr. Nobukuki Kawata

Julie Chait

Dr. Jaime Moriguchi

Roella Minkley

Dr. Hillel Laks

Shelly Ruzevich

Dr. Davis Drinkwater

Caron Utley

Dr. Antoine Hage

Jerrine and Jane

Dr. Anne Peters

Debbie and Arlene

Dr. Katherine Fallick

Lelia and Julie

Dr. Jane Frye

Betty Palmer

Sheryl Hines
for her input in the design of this book

Barbara Olvera
for her designing talent and technical support

Sue Bugden
for her syntactical and grammatical assistance

Elisha Teems
from Esha Research

and to Janis
for her unconditional love

Foreword

Organ transplant programs are created to fill a very real need—to prolong the lives of people needing new hearts for their survival. The UCLA Transplant Program performed its first heart transplant in February 1984, and as of May 1999, we have given new lives to more than 918 men, women, and children from newborn to 74 years of age. Working closely with organizations who find donor hearts across the country, UCLA has proudly become the largest heart transplant program in the United States.

With each new medical advance...with each new surgical advance...and with each new pharmaceutical advance, the transplantation procedure and follow-up become that much safer and that much more successful. But all the advances are useless without the lifesaving decision by the families of the donors. These courageous people make our work and the miracle of transplantation possible.

All the recipes in this book have been designed to fall within appropriate "heart-healthy" boundaries.

Each has fewer than 500 calories, contains less than 200 mg of cholesterol, has less than 200 mg of sodium, and less than 30 percent of its calories are derived from fat.

I hope you enjoy every one of the dishes. The book was written by one of our heart transplant patients, who, as a direct result of organ transplantation, has had a chance to write and contribute to society.

It is hoped that someday soon you will join many millions of Americans and sign your donor card.

Jon Kobashigawa, M.D. *Associate Clinical Professor of Medicine, UCLA School of Medicine*
Medical Director, UCLA Heart Transplant Program

Contents

All recipes in this book are below 500 calories, contain less than 200 mg of cholesterol, have less than 200 mg of sodium, and have less than 30% of their calories from fat.

Introduction

In June 1993, I received the transplanted heart of a donor I'd never meet, never know anything about or ever be able to thank.

I told myself that if a donor was willing to help me continue a productive life, I'd help others by encouraging them to eat properly prepared healthy meals.

I'm not a professional chef. Nobody's paying me to endorse his or her products. That said, allow me to answer some soon-to-be-asked questions.

Jeffrey, if you're not a professional chef, how do you know all this stuff?

I've had an interest in food and its preparation for as long as I can remember. During my summers in high school and college I worked in a snack bar at a beach club in Mamaroneck, New York. I learned some things there that have stuck with me all these years. I've represented many restaurants during my twenty-some years in advertising. Some of the restaurants were ethnic, some were elegant, one was a cozy jazz spot; one was even a link in a fast-food chain. I loved to talk to the owners and chefs at these restaurants. I helped myself to as many questions as I could think of. The more questions I asked (and were answered), the more time I spent watching and the more little tidbits I learned. All the hints and tips throughout the book come from these learned ladies and gentlemen.

Why did you choose chicken?

I had my choice of several high-protein, low-cholesterol meats to feature—chicken, fish, pork, even lean beef. I could tell you I chose chicken because we've been eating chicken for thousands of years in thousands of different ways in thousands of different places all over the world.

Or I could tell you the truth: I like chicken the best. How's that for a medically based decision?

The secret of great cooking: Know what goes in the pot first, what goes in last, and that it's alright to be creative in between.

As my grandmother would say, "Enjoy."

Where did you get all these recipes?

I searched through old dusty cookbooks, poured through yellowed magazine recipes taped in loose-leaf notebooks, asked friends and their families, scoured used-bookstores, and even found a few on the internet; I searched anywhere and everywhere I might find chicken recipes. You'll recognize many of them by their names and ingredients. They are, after all, "classics."

Along the way, working with good people, I created some new recipes that are healthier, and, believe it or not, just as enjoyable as the fatty, high-calorie, high-cholesterol, salty original ones.

Where did you get all those numbers at the bottom of the recipes?

All nutritional analysis comes from the ESHA *Food Processor* program, version 2.2. *Food Processor* is used by more than 5,000 hospitals, colleges, and professional dieticians and nutritionists throughout the world.

Any more questions? Write me. If I don't know the answers I'll find them and get back to you.

—Jeffrey

HANDLING CHICKEN

❦Before cleaning, rub the chicken with lemon juice. This will eliminate any odors.

❦For the healthiest cooking, remove all fat from the chicken, including the skin. You can always add a spritz of nonfat spray if you're concerned about losing moisture during cooking.

❦Always buy grade A chicken. It makes no difference whether it's yellow or white.

❦Always stuff chicken loosely. The stuffing will expand as it cooks, which will ensure the stuffing stays inside!

❦Follow this rule of thumb for stuffing: one cup of dry stuffing per pound of chicken.

❦Always season the cavity of the chicken as well as the outside.

❦Always remove stuffing immediately after your meal to avoid food poisoning when freezing leftover stuffed chicken.

❦To absorb fat from chicken stock, place a lettuce leaf in the pot. Remove it as soon as it's done its job.

❦To thicken sauces, use cornstarch or arrowroot instead of flour, both of which are also better for weight control.

❦When freezing chicken pieces to prevent sticking, place them on a cookie sheet, let them freeze completely, then put them in plastic bags.

❦For marinating, use only glass or plastic containers, which lessen the possibility of food contamination.

❦When using marinades as basting sauces, apply them only during the last 5 minutes of grilling or broiling, or baste only during the final 30 minutes of cooking. The sauce will not penetrate the meat during the early stages, which may cause chicken to brown too quickly.

❦The best way to determine whether your chicken is done is to place a meat thermometer in the thickest part of the chicken's thigh away from the bone. If the thermometer reads 165°–170° the chicken's done.

❦When sautéing boneless chicken breasts or other chicken pieces, use a shallow skillet if you want the chicken to remain crisp. A deep pan creates steam, causing a buildup of moisture and a loss of crispness.

❦When cooking, use only homemade chicken stock. It's simple to make. There's an easy-to-prepare recipe on page 11 for you. If you must use prepared stock, buy only those that have been defatted and are unsalted. If you cannot find unsalted stock, substitute water. This is very critical.

❦Grill chicken on medium coals. If you can hold your hand over the grill for a count of four, the coals are medium.

❦Never crowd your skillet. It affects cooking times and doesn't allow your chicken to cook properly. Try not to let the chicken pieces touch one another. They'll come out better if you cook them in two batches.

❦Any spices mentioned in the recipes are completely up to you and your taste. If you're brave, increase the chili powder or use less if you're a little shy. Make yourself happy!

❦Taste-test recipes during cooking. If more spice blend or pepper is needed, add them.

❦ Don't let your garlic brown when using it to flavor oils. It becomes bitter and will affect the taste of the dish.

❦I haven't mentioned the s-word (salt) in any of the recipes. You know it's bad for you…and we both know you're going to be tempted to use it anyhow. Please be judicious! We want you to stay around.

❦All applicable nutiritional numbers are based on the recipe for chicken stock on page 11 in this book. Numbers will change dramatically if whole soy sauce or canned chicken broth is used.

❦Finally: When you go to a restaurant, always ask for a table near a waiter.

ROASTING GARLIC

When garlic is roasted until it's buttery soft, it becomes sweet and delicate tasting.

Squeezing each roasted clove will extract the soft flesh from the skin. This is delicious spread on bread sprinkled with a dash of my spice blend and freshly ground pepper.

Roasted garlic is wonderful added to sauces, soups, sandwich spreads, and salad dressings for additional flavor.

Here's a simple, low-fat preparation.

1. Cut head of garlic vertically ⅓ down from the top. Drizzle ¼-teaspoon olive oil on top of exposed cloves on both halves.
2. Wrap each firm, plump garlic head in foil, twisting the foil closed at the top.
3. Place the packets on a baking sheet.
4. Roast in a 400° oven one hour.

If you own a garlic roaster, simply follow the directions, but watch the amount of oil you use.

GRILLING THE MIDDLE-EASTERN WAY

Serve the grilled chicken with pita bread, rice pilaf, and lemon wedges.

1. Make sure you wash the chicken well. If using boneless chicken pieces, cut them into 1-inch cubes and place in a shallow, nonreactive container. If using whole chicken, leave broiler halves whole.

2. Select one of the marinades on page 6, then combine the ingredients in a bowl, pour over the chicken, cover, and marinate it in the refrigerator overnight.

3. Bring the meat to room temperature before cooking. While it is warming, prepare a fire in a charcoal grill or preheat a broiler.

4. Remove the meat from the marinade, reserving the marinade. If using cubed chicken, thread onto skewers. Place the skewers, butterflied, or halved chicken on the grill rack (or on a broiler pan). Grill (or broil) until cooked through, basting with the marinade while cooking. Cooking time will depend on the size of the chicken pieces. Do not let the meat become dry.

MIDDLE-EASTERN MARINADES

Lebanese Marinade
4 to 6 cloves finely minced garlic
½ cup fresh lemon juice
2 teaspoons chopped fresh thyme
1 teaspoon paprika
¼ to ½ teaspoon cayenne pepper (optional)
½ teaspoon freshly ground black pepper
½ cup olive oil

Turkish Marinade
1 cup plain yogurt
1 tablespoon paprika
1 teaspoon ground cinnamon or
1 tablespoon ground cumin
¼ teaspoon cayenne pepper, or to taste
4 cloves minced garlic
Juice of 1 lemon
6 tablespoons olive oil
½ teaspoon freshly ground black pepper
½ cup grated onion

Moroccan Marinade
1 tablespoon paprika
2 teaspoons ground cumin
½ teaspoon cayenne pepper
1 teaspoon ground ginger
½ cup melted unsalted butter or olive oil
Juice of 1 large lemon
Freshly ground pepper to taste

Egyptian Marinade
½ cup olive oil
2 tablespoons ground cumin
1 tablespoon ground coriander
1 grated onion
3 cloves finely minced garlic
1 teaspoon cayenne pepper
Freshly ground pepper to taste

DRY-RUB MARINADES

Here are three especially good, classic international dry-rub marinades.

Greek Marinade
> *¼ cup oregano, chopped*
> *2 tablespoons mint, chopped*
> *1 tablespoon dill*
> *½ teaspoon cinnamon*
> *½ teaspoon allspice*

French Marinade
> *2 tablespoons basil, chopped*
> *2 tablespoons thyme, chopped*
> *2 tablespoons savory, chopped*
> *1 tablespoon fennel seeds*

Italian Marinade
> *3 tablespoons oregano, chopped*
> *3 tablespoons basil, chopped*
> *1 teaspoon rosemary, chopped*
> *2 teaspoons sage, chopped*
> *1 tablespoon marjoram, chopped*

SIMPLE TIPS FOR BETTER-TASTING FOOD
(From the restaurants of my past)

❦Remove the skin from chicken and any pads of fat you find.

❦Grind your own pepper for maximum flavor.

❦Use fresh herbs when possible. Crumble them in your hand before adding them to a dish. This will release the full, true flavor of the seasoning.

❦Use fresh lemons, limes, oranges, and fruits whenever possible.

❦Make your own bread crumbs—they're tastier and much healthier for you.

❦To remove the saltiness from feta cheese, and from anchovies, let them sit for a while in a bowl of milk before using them. (Don't forget to throw out the milk.)

❦Use fresh food whenever possible. If you must use canned or packaged foods, please read the labels carefully!

HELPFUL KITCHEN HINTS

❦To ensure a ready supply of garlic, whiz several heads in a food processor, mold into a log shape and roll it in plastic wrap. Give it a second wrapping of aluminum foil and hide it in the freezer. When you're ready to use it, just lop off a slice and return the rest to the freezer.

❦Before slicing boneless chicken or turkey breast, place it in the freezer about 20 minutes. This makes it firm and easier to trim and slice.

❦For a continuous supply of zest, always grate the peel of oranges, lemons, limes, and grapefruit before squeezing the juice from them. Package the grated peel in small containers or foil packs, and freeze for later use.

❦To make citrus fruits juicier, place them in a colander and run hot tap water over them a few minutes. Then roll them around on the counter with pressure from the palm of your hand before juicing.

❦To remove garlic, onion, or fish odors from your hands, rub them with vinegar or lemon juice and rinse in cold water.

❦⅓ or ½ teaspoon of dried herb equals 1 tablespoon of fresh herb.

❦½ pound of fresh mushrooms amounts to 2½ cups.

❦One slice of bread yields ¾ cup of soft bread crumbs.

❦Plunge hard-boiled eggs immediately into cold water. This will prevent the yolks from turning dark.

❦If you want a really crisp salad, wash the lettuce leaves, wrap in a linen cloth, and refrigerate for ½ hour or so.

❦Cutting the white tendon that runs lengthwise on a boneless chicken breast will keep the breast from shrinking as much during cooking.

❦ For delicious stuffing, use only peeled, cored apples. Stuff your chicken and enjoy the apples.

It really does pay to have good knives. Buy the best you can afford, but don't hesitate to splurge. They'll last years.

JEFFREY'S SECRET SPICE BLEND

All chefs, it seems, have a secret spice blend. Here's mine. Use it as a salt substitute as it is, or you can vary the amounts and choice of spices to create your own. A nutritional extra of this recipe is that it adds no additional calories, fats, or sodium.

This will get you started:

> 2 tablespoons chili powder
> 2 teaspoons fennel seed, ground
> 2 teaspoons mustard seed, ground
> 1 teaspoon cayenne pepper
> 1 teaspoon cinnamon
> 1 teaspoon dried mint
> 1 teaspoon dill weed
> 1 tablespoon black pepper
> 1 tablespoon onion powder
> 1 tablespoon garlic powder
> 2 tablespoons sweet paprika
> 1 teaspoon ground cumin

PERFECTLY HEALTHY CHICKEN STOCK

Chicken stock is so much more than a base for soups and sauces. It's also a perfect poaching liquid for both chicken and vegetables. Even rice or pasta made in a rich stock will taste much better. Here's an easy recipe for a homemade stock. Because all the fat is skimmed and it contains no added salt, it's nutritional content is minimal.

> *1 bouquet garni consisting of*
> *2 bay leaves*
> *1 large yellow or white onion*
> *4 whole cloves*
> *15–20 parsley stems…no leaves*
> *1–2 cloves of garlic*
> *2 stalks of celery*
> *2 whole carrots, peeled and cut into 4 pieces each*
> *2 parsnips peeled and cut into 3 pieces each*
> *1 large leek (white part only)*
> *4 fresh pea pods*
> *One 5–7 pound roasting chicken, skinned,*
> *16 cups cold water*

1. Place contents of the bouquet garni inside a piece of cheese-cloth and wrap with string.
2. Thoroughly wash the chicken, removing all visible fat.
3. Place the chicken in a large stockpot or kettle and add the cold water.
4. Bring to a boil quickly and then reduce heat and simmer gently.
5. Add bouquet garni tying one end of the string to the pot handle (easier to find and remove later).
6. Adjust the heat so that the liquid just bubbles. Do not allow it to come to a boil again.
7. Skim off the foam that accumulates on the surface as the stock simmers.
8. Cook uncovered 1½–2 hours.

9. When done, the meat should fall off the bones, but the bones should remain whole.
10. Turn off heat and remove chicken and bouquet garni.
11. Throw out bouquet garni and set aside chicken until cooled.
12. Strain stock through a colander lined with several layers of dampened cheesecloth.

If you're not going to use the stock immediately, allow to cool to room temperature, refrigerate, and remove fat that comes to the top while refrigerated. Separate the chicken meat from the bones and use another time (it makes a nice chicken salad).

The stock may be kept in sealed jars in the refrigerator 3–5 days, or may be frozen in serving-size containers about 6 months.

The
RECIPES

AFELIA
(CYPRUS)

Here's a thousand-year-old recipe. Enjoy it with a nice salad and pita bread.

1½ pounds chicken breasts, skinless, boneless, and diced
7 ounces red wine
1–2 tablespoons coarsely crushed coriander seeds
pinch of spice blend and lots of freshly ground black pepper
1 cinnamon stick
1 tablespoon vegetable oil

1. Marinate the chicken in the wine and spices for at least 4 hours, or overnight, if possible.
2. Remove the chicken from the marinade and dry with kitchen paper towel.
3. Reserve the marinade for later.
4. Heat the oil in a heavy-based casserole. Brown the chicken a few pieces at a time until they're crispy brown.
5. Wipe any excess oil from the pan and return the chicken.
6. Pour the marinade and enough cold water over the meat to just cover it. Cover the casserole with a lid and cook about 30 minutes or until the meat is tender. Almost all the liquid should have evaporated to leave a thick sauce. If necessary, cook the dish uncovered another 10 minutes to reduce any excess liquid.

Serves 4
Calories per serving 272
Cholesterol, mg 98.6
Calories from fat, % 19
Sodium 115

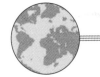

Enjoy the influences of India and Asia. Serve these kabobs with basmati rice.

AFGHAN KABOBS

2 pounds chicken breasts, boneless, skinless
1 cup plain low-fat yogurt
3 tablespoons lemon juice
1 tablespoon canola oil
1 tablespoon minced garlic
¾ teaspoon freshly ground pepper
Spice blend to taste

1. Cut chicken into ¾" pieces.
2. Place remaining ingredients in large bowl. Add chicken to marinade, toss well coating all pieces.
3. Cover and marinate at room temperature 2 hours or up to 2 days in the refrigerator.
4. Remove chicken from refrigerator at least 1 hour before cooking. Thread meat along skewers.
5. Wait until charcoal has reached a white ash consistency and heat is moderate.
6. Grill, turning skewers 3 times, until meat is cooked, about 10–20 minutes.
7. Slide kabobs onto heated platter.

Serves 6

Calories per serving 216
Cholesterol, mg 90.1
Calories from fat, % 21
Sodium, mg 127

AFRICAN

3–4-pound chicken, cut into 8 pieces
⅓ cup yellow onion
½ teaspoon dill weed
½ cup low-fat peanut butter (creamy or chunky)
3 tablespoons cornstarch
½ cup water

1. Pierce chicken pieces.
2. Place in large pot with onion and dill. Cover with water.
3. Bring to boil, reduce heat, and simmer 40 minutes.
4. Mix peanut butter with ½ cup of stock from pot.
5. Return mixture to the pot.
6. Dissolve cornstarch in ½ cup water. Mix into pot, making the sauce.

Africans love groundnuts. We call them peanuts. Serve this chicken over a heaping helping of brown rice, browned onions, pineapple, and toasted coconut.

Serves 6
Calories per serving 378
Cholesterol, mg 135
Calories from fat, % 28
Sodium, mg 165

*(Dramatic desert music, in
the background over which
we hear an imposing voice.)
"From the vast Sahara desert
in the North of Africa…"
This is complete when served
over couscous.*

ALGERIAN

*1 pound chicken breasts, boneless, skinless
1 medium onion, sliced and separated into rings
2 garlic cloves, minced
2 tablespoons olive oil
4 chopped tomatoes
2 medium carrots cut into 1" slices
2 celery stalks, cut into 1" slices
1 medium turnip, peeled and cubed
1 medium zucchini cut into 1" pieces
½ cup raisins*

1. In 12" skillet, sauté garlic and onion in oil. Remove mixture set aside.
2. In same pan, brown chicken pieces on all sides over medium heat.
3. Drain off fat.
4. Return onion rings to pan. Add tomatoes, carrots, celery, and turnip.
5. Reduce heat, cover, and simmer 30 minutes. Stir zucchini and raisins into mixture.
6. Cover and simmer another 10 minutes.

Turnip

Serves 4
Calories per serving 333
Cholesterol, mg 65.7
Calories from fat, % 23
Sodium, mg 138

AMARETTO

4 chicken breasts, skinless and boneless (4–6 ounces each)
2 tablespoons flour
Spice blend
1½ teaspoons freshly ground black pepper
1 tablespoon vegetable oil
2 tablespoons unsalted butter
1 tablespoon Dijon mustard
6 ounces fresh orange juice
4 ounces Amaretto

1. Preheat oven to 350°.
2. Mix the can of frozen orange juice with a half can of water.
3. Combine flour, pepper, and paprika.
4. Coat chicken with this mixture.
5. Heat oil and unsalted butter in skillet and sauté chicken until brown.
6. Remove and put in casserole. Turn off heat under skillet
7. Add mustard, orange juice, and Amaretto. (Watch out for flames.)
8. Increase heat and boil, stirring constantly, until thick.
9. Pour sauce over chicken and bake, covered, 45 minutes.

This dish can be frozen and reheated later.

Sound Italian? French? Spanish? Who cares? It's tasty, easy to make, and a perfect excuse to serve green beans and almonds!

Serves 4
Calories per serving 480
Cholesterol, mg 136
Calories from fat, % 28
Sodium, mg 172

During the eighteenth and nineteenth centuries, German immigrants settled in Pennsylvania and Ohio. They brought with them a work ethic and an austerity that remains to this day. Serve this tasty dish with mashed potatoes and mixed vegetables.

AMISH OVEN BAKED

4 pounds skinless chicken breasts
3 tablespoons canola oil
1 cup flour
1 teaspoon spice blend
2 teaspoons freshly ground pepper
2 teaspoons marjoram

1. Pre heat oven to 375°.
2. Rub chicken pieces with the oil.
3. Put remaining ingredients in a brown paper bag.
4. Add chicken pieces to bag and toss to make sure all pieces are covered.
5. Let chicken pieces stand one hour.
6. Place chicken on cooking sheet; bake 45 minutes.
7. Turn and bake additional 15 minutes.

Serves 8
Calories per serving 495
Cholesterol, mg 180
Calories from fat, % 21
Sodium, mg 164

Marjoram

ANGLO-SAXON

4–5-pound chicken
2 ounces unsalted butter
1 pound leeks, washed, trimmed and thickly sliced
4 cloves finely chopped garlic
6 ounces barley
3¾ cups water
3 generous tablespoons red or white wine vinegar
2 bay leaves
Spice blend, pepper to taste
15 fresh sage leaves, roughly chopped

1. Melt the butter in a heavy pan and sauté the meat with the leeks and garlic until the vegetables are slightly softened and the meat lightly browned. Add the barley, water, vinegar, bay leaves, and seasoning.
2. Bring the pot to the boil, cover it, and simmer gently for 1–1½ hours or until the meat is really tender and ready to fall from the bone.
3. Add the sage and continue to cook for several minutes.
4. Adjust the seasoning to taste and serve in bowls—the barley is the vegetable.

In seventh-century England, herbs were one of the few flavorings available to cooks and were used heavily. Add crusty bread and you've got a complete meal.

Serves 6
Calories per serving 316
Cholesterol, mg . . . . 84.
Calories from fat, % 30
Sodium, mg 95.7

The perfect dinner for a fall evening. Serve with a side dish of squash and a crisp salad.

APPLE CHICKEN

1½ pounds chicken breasts, boneless, skinless
½ cup apple cider
3 tablespoons apple butter
1 teaspoon lemon rind, grated
1 tablespoon lemon juice
½ teaspoon spice blend
1½ tablespoons canola oil
1 small onion, thinly sliced
1 small apple, cored
1 teaspoon cornstarch
2 tablespoons walnuts, chopped and toasted
Apple wedges and sage for garnish (optional)

1. Combine first four ingredients in a bowl, stir well, and set aside.
2. Sprinkle chicken with spice blend.
3. Coat a large nonstick skillet with cooking spray; place over medium high heat until hot.
4. Add chicken, cook 5 minutes on each side or until browned. Remove, drain on paper towels. Wipe drippings from pan, return chicken to pan.
5. Pour cider mixture over chicken, and top with onion slices.
6. Cover, reduce heat, and simmer 10 minutes.
7. Add 12 apple wedges.
8. Cover and simmer 12 minutes or until chicken is tender.
9. Transfer chicken and apple wedges to a serving platter with a slotted spoon. Dissolve cornstarch in water in a small bowl.
10. Add to cider mixture in pan, stirring constantly, until mixture is thickened.
11. Spoon sauce over chicken and sprinkle with walnuts. If desired, garnish with apple wedges and sage sprigs.

Serves 6

Calories per serving 316
Cholesterol, mg 84.3
Calories from fat, % 30
Sodium, mg 95.7

APRICOT FLAVORED
(DELHI)

5-pound chicken, skinned and cut into small pieces
4 whole dried hot red chilies
2" cinnamon stick, broken in half
1 teaspoon each cumin seeds and crushed garlic
7 cardamon pods and 10 cloves
2 teaspoons grated ginger
4 ounces pitted, dried apricots
4 tablespoons vegetable oil
1 pound onions, cut in very fine half rings
2 tablespoons tomato puree in 8 ounces hot water
1 pint water
Pinch of spice blend
2 tablespoons malt vinegar
1 tablespoon sugar

1. Put red chilies, cinnamon, cumin, cardamon, and cloves in a grinder and grind finely.
2. Put chicken in a big bowl. Sprinkle on 1 teaspoon grated ginger, ½ teaspoon garlic, and half the dry spice mix. Mix well, rubbing seasoning into the chicken. Set aside 1 hour.
3. Place apricots into a pan with 1 pint of water. Boil, reduce heat, and simmer until tender, but not mushy. Turn off the heat and marinate in juice.
4. Heat oil in a pan over medium heat. Add onions, stir, and sauté until rich brown.
5. Add rest of garlic, ginger, and dry spice mix. Stir, add chicken, and brown 5 minutes.
6. Add tomato puree mix and spice blend. Boil, cover, reduce heat, and simmer 20 minutes. Add vinegar and sugar, Cover, simmer 10 minutes. Turn off heat. Spoon off as much fat as possible.
7. Add apricots and 3 tablespoons of juice to chicken. Let sit a half hour before serving.

This isn't the "delhi" food you thought it was! This northern Indian dish is terrific with Basmati rice and a cool riata.

Serves 6
Calories per serving 247
Cholesterol, mg 90.6
Calories from fat, % 30
Sodium, mg 104

Credit the Moors for some of the intricate taste in Spanish cuisine. They brought the spices of the Orient as well as fruit, almond and olive trees. The cumin in this dish creates a faint Oriental flavor. Serve with rice and crusty bread.

ARAGON
(SPAIN)

6 4-ounce chicken breasts, skinless, boneless
3 Spanish onions, sliced
1 clove garlic, minced
2 tablespoons extra virgin olive oil (Spanish, if possible)
4 ounces chicken broth
4 ounces sherry (Spanish, if possible)
¼ teaspoon cumin
2 ounces half-and-half
1 tablespoon fresh parsley, chopped

1. Heat the oil in a skillet, and when hot, add chicken breasts. Brown well on both sides.
2. Add the sliced onion and garlic. Cook until slightly browned and add broth, sherry, and cumin.
3. Cover and cook over low heat 20 minutes or until the breasts are tender.
4. Remove the chicken to a serving platter and keep warm.
5. Pour the sauce and onions into a blender or food processor and blend until the sauce is smooth.
6. Return sauce to skillet and cook until heated through.
7. Add the cream and mix well.
8. Pour the sauce over the chicken and sprinkle the chopped parsley on top.

Serves 6
Calories per serving 214
Cholesterol, mg 68.9
Calories from fat, % 30
Sodium, mg 84.8

ARROZ CON POLLO
(MADRID-STYLE)

1½ pounds chicken breasts, boneless, skinless
1 tablespoon unsalted butter
1 tablespoon canola oil
2 cloves minced garlic
¼ teaspoon ground pepper
¼ teaspoon paprika
¼ cup each diced onion and green pepper
2 cups uncooked rice
1 cup each chicken stock and water
½ cup chopped fresh tomatoes
⅛ teaspoon turmeric
½ cup fresh green peas

1. Preheat oven to 350°.
2. Rinse chicken, pat dry, set aside.
3. In small saucepan, on medium heat, melt butter. Add garlic, black pepper, and paprika. Mix well, remove from heat, and brush mixture on chicken.
4. Place chicken in ovenproof dish. Bake uncovered 20–25 minutes or until meat has turned white.
5. In large nonstick skillet on medium heat, sauté onion and green pepper in oil for 5 minutes.
6. Add rice and cook another 2–3 minutes, stirring frequently. Add water, chicken stock, tomatoes, and turmeric. Stir, cover, and simmer on low heat 20–25 minutes.
7. Add peas and chicken. Cook an additional 10 minutes.

There are as many recipes for this famous dish as there are chefs preparing it. Feel free to add your own touch, but keep it healthy.

Serves 6
Calories per serving 380
Cholesterol, mg 167
Calories from fat, % 14
Sodium, mg 188

Eastern Europe played host to everyone from the Mongols to the Romans and that means multilevel cuisine. Lucky us! All this needs is crusty peasant bread.

AUSTRIAN

2 pounds chicken breasts, skinless
2 pounds thighs, skinless
1 cup Riesling or other fruity white wine
¼ cup shallots, minced
2 sprigs fresh thyme (or ¼ teaspoon dried)
Spice blend, pepper to taste
1 slice of bacon, chopped
16 pearl onions
3 turnips peeled and diced
2 carrots, diced
8 large mushrooms, quartered
⅔ cup chicken stock
1 tablespoon fresh tarragon (or 1 teaspoon dried)

1. Combine chicken, wine, shallots, thyme in large bowl. Toss well, and refrigerate overnight.
2. Remove chicken pieces, reserving marinade. Pat chicken pieces dry, season with spice blend and pepper.
3. Cook chopped bacon in heavy skillet or casserole until crisp. Drain on paper towel.
4. Add chicken to skillet, cook over medium heat until golden brown, about 3 minutes per side.
5. Add bacon, onion, turnip, carrots, and mushrooms. Cover and cook until tender, about 15 minutes. Arrange on platter, keep warm.
6. Add reserved marinade and stock to skillet. Boil until reduced to ¾ cup.
7. Defat sauce. Stir in tarragon, spoon over chicken.

Serves 6
Calories per serving 323
Cholesterol, mg 111
Calories from fat, % 9
Sodium, mg 189

AUTUMN CHICKEN

16 ounces chicken breasts, boneless,
*   skinless, cut into thin strips*
3 cups onion, chopped
1 tablespoon garlic, minced
2 teaspoons ground cumin
1 teaspoon ground cinnamon
½ teaspoon ground tumeric
¼ teaspoon chili powder
2 pounds tomatoes
2 cups corn kernels (fresh is best)
1 cup plain nonfat yogurt
1 teaspoon cornstarch

1. Sauté onions in hot oil in a large nonstick skillet. Add garlic, ginger, cumin, turmeric, chili powder, and cinnamon. Stir well and continue cooking over medium heat.
2. Wash and chop tomatoes into chunks. Stir into onion and spice mixture. Continue cooking.
3. Wash and dry chicken pieces and add to skillet. Add corn. Cook 5–6 minutes.
4. Mix a small amount of the yogurt with the cornstarch until smooth, then blend with the remaining yogurt. Stir into skillet and cook until mixture thickens—just a couple of minutes.
5. Season with spice blend and pepper.

Talk about color matching taste. Serve over white rice and enjoy.

Serves 4

Calories per serving 320
Cholesterol, mg 52.5
Calories from fat, % 19
Sodium, mg 132

A combination of Brazilian, Portuguese, and African influences in one dish. Serve with white rice seasoned with cayenne pepper, peas, chopped onion, and thyme.

BAHIAN

1 pound chicken breasts, skinless, boneless, cut into pieces
1 tablespoon olive oil
1 cup onion, sliced
1 cup green pepper, sliced
8 ounces tomato puree
4 ounces water
thyme (to taste)

1. Lightly brown chicken pieces in hot oil, adding the onion, green pepper, and a small amount of spice blend and pepper.
2. Pour tomato puree over chicken and dilute with water.
3. Sprinkle with thyme.
4. Cover and steam over medium heat 20–25 minutes.

Serves 4

Calories per serving 157
Cholesterol, mg 51
Calories from fat, % 15
Sodium, mg 84.8

Thyme

BEIJING CHESTNUT CHICKEN

3 pounds chicken pieces, skinned
6 dried Chinese black mushrooms
8-ounce can water chestnuts, drained and sliced
1 tablespoon minced ginger
2 tablespoons canola oil
2 cups water
3 tablespoons low-sodium soy sauce
2 tablespoons rice wine (or sherry)

1. Soak dried mushrooms in warm water 30 minutes. Rinse and cut in half, set aside. Discard liquid
2. Heat oil in heavy skillet and quickly brown chicken pieces.
3. Add ginger and mushrooms. Stir-fry 1 minute.
4. Meanwhile, heat, but do not boil water. Stir in soy sauce and rice wine. Pour over chicken and bring to a boil.
5. Cover and simmer chicken 30–35 minutes.
6. Add chestnuts. Cover and simmer an additional 15 minutes.

No longer a Forbidden City meal! Serve on a bed of steamed white rice.

Serves 6

Calories per serving 185
Cholesterol, mg 79.5
Calories from fat, % 27
Sodium, mg 175

A "me'jum curry ol' thing!"
Serve on a bed of basmati
rice, and try an authentic
chutney.

BENGAL LIME CURRY

4 chicken breasts, boneless, skinless
2 teaspoons olive oil
2 shallots, thinly sliced
¼ cup green bell pepper, diced
1 tablespoon curry powder (or to taste)
Juice of 2 limes
¼ cup plain low-fat yogurt
Parsley sprigs and slivered almonds for garnish

1. Cut chicken diagonally into thin slices.
2. In a large, nonstick skillet, heat oil and sauté shallots until soft.
3. Add bell pepper and cook until tender. Stir in curry powder.
4. Add chicken and stir-fry 2–3 minutes. Add lime juice.
5. Just before serving, stir yogurt into skillet.
6. Garnish with parsley and slivered almonds.

Parsley

Serves 4

Calories per serving 173
Cholesterol, mg 69.3
Calories from fat, % 22
Sodium, mg 88

BIG SKY CASSEROLE

4-pound chicken, skinless, cut into 8 pieces
4 tablespoons flour
1 tablespoon spice blend
Freshly grated ginger to taste
6 carrots, peeled and quartered
2 ounces unsalted butter
1 cup water
1½ cups chicken stock
1 tablespoon catsup
½ tablespoon Worcestershire sauce
2 bay leaves
6 small onions, peeled
6 potatoes, peeled and quartered
8 ounces mushrooms
16 ounces fresh peas

1. Preheat oven to 350°.
2. Mix flour, spice blend, pepper, and ginger, and dredge chicken pieces in the mix.
3. Brown the dredged chicken in a skillet with melted butter.
4. Remove pieces when brown and save the drippings.
5. Put chicken pieces in a large casserole.
6. Add flour to the drippings, making a paste.
7. Stir in water, stock, catsup, Worcestershire sauce, bay leaves, and onions.
8. Pour over chicken and bake 45 minutes.
9. Add potatoes, carrots, and mushrooms. Bake 35 minutes more. Add peas and bake 10 minutes longer.

This one's from Wyoming. I needed a name that started with B. I changed it. Sue me! It's a complete meal, especially when you add a lot of stars.

Serves 6

Calories per serving 491
Cholesterol, mg 115
Calories from fat, % 29
Sodium, mg 145

From the western coast of this exotic civilization. The mango cools this dish down…so will a side of basmati rice.

BOMBAY
(INDIA)

1½ pounds chicken breasts, skinless,
 boneless, cut into pieces,
2 tablespoons olive oil
2 tablespoons butter
2 large sliced onions
2 cloves garlic, finely minced
3 large, ripe mangoes, peeled
¼ teaspoon ground nutmeg
½ teaspoon ground turmeric
¼ teaspoon freshly ground pepper
Spice blend to taste
Juice of 1 lemon
1 cup chicken stock
Zest of ½ lemon, cut into strips

1. Heat 3 tablespoons of olive oil in large saucepan on medium high.
2. Sauté chicken until lightly browned. Remove and drain over pan.
3. Reduce heat, add butter and remainder of oil to pan. Sauté onions and garlic until tender.
4. Roughly chop and add half of mangoes. Season with nutmeg, spice blend, pepper, and turmeric. Add lemon zest.
5. Cook, stirring 2 minutes.
6. Return chicken to pan with stock. Cover pan and simmer 45 minutes or until tender. Put chicken in casserole and keep in warm oven.
7. Reduce mango gravy in pan by one-half. Stir in lemon juice, stirring another 5 minutes. Pour over chicken.
8. Slice remaining mangoes crosswise and arrange over chicken. Allow to warm in oven another 10–15 minutes.

Serves 6

Calories per serving 270
Cholesterol, mg 70.9
Calories from fat, % 27
Sodium, mg 77.3

BRAZILIAN

8 chicken breasts, boned and skinned (6 ounces each)
½ cup orange juice
¼ cup lemon juice
¼ cup Dijon mustard
⅛ cup olive oil
⅛ cup honey
2 cloves garlic, minced
Zested rinds of 1 orange and 1 lemon
1 sprig fresh rosemary

1. Preheat oven to 350°.
2. Mix ingredients, add chicken, and marinate overnight.
3. Bake one hour or until tender.

Rosemary

African influences are all over Brazil. Serve this with Latin-American-style couscous made with cornmeal and fresh vegetables.

Serves 6
Calories per serving 231
Cholesterol, mg 68.4
Calories from fat, % 26
Sodium, mg 166

A simple baked potato is perfect with this simple all-American dish.

BREASTS WITH LEEKS AND ORANGES

6 chicken breasts, skinless and boneless, pounded to
  ¼" thickness
12 leeks
2 tablespoons canola oil
Juice and zest of 2 oranges
1 tablespoon unsalted butter, melted
Pepper to taste
1 cup fresh mint leaves

1. Cut leeks into the same size as the breasts.
2. Boil leeks in lightly spiced blended water 10 minutes. Drain.
3. Heat half the oil, add leeks, and sauté. Add one-half of zest and juice to the leeks. Cover and simmer on low heat 15 minutes.
4. "Paint" the chicken with melted unsalted butter, sprinkle with pepper and remaining orange zest.
5. In each breast, place 3 mint leaves in center and 1 leek crosswise. Roll and tie.
6. Sauté breasts in remaining oil until brown, 15–20 minutes. Remove and keep warm.
7. Turn heat to high and simmer sauce 7 minutes. Add the remaining mint. Pour over chicken and serve.

Serves 6
Calories per serving 253
Cholesterol, mg 73.2
Calories from fat, % 29
Sodium, mg 103

BURMESE CASSEROLE

3 pounds chicken breasts, skinless
1 tablespoon canola oil
2 cloves garlic, chopped
2 tablespoons green onions, chopped
1 tablespoon ginger, grated
1 cup mushrooms, sliced
3 ounces chicken stock
3 ounces water
½ cup Chinese rice wine (or sherry)
¾ tablespoon low-sodium soy sauce
½ teaspoon sugar
1 teaspoon coriander

1. Brown chicken pieces in oil.
2. In Dutch oven, sauté garlic, ginger, green onions, and mushrooms.
3. Add chicken, stock, water, sherry, soy, sugar and coriander. Cover and simmer 1½ hours.

Burmese cooking is somewhere between Cambodian and Indonesian in "heat." Enjoy this dish with a cooling cucumber salad.

Green Onion

Serves 8
Calories per serving 228
Cholesterol, mg 98.6
Calories from fat, % 15
Sodium, mg 159

Cajun cooking can be as hot as you want it. Tame this one down with red beans and rice.

CAJUN OVEN BAKED

3–4 pounds chicken pieces, skinned
¼ teaspoon curry powder
¼ teaspoon ground cumin
¼ teaspoon ground oregano
¼ teaspoon paprika
¼ teaspoon crushed red pepper
½ teaspoon garlic powder
½ cup arrowroot
¼ cup yellow cornmeal
½ cup nonfat buttermilk
1 tablespoon Worcestershire sauce
1 tablespoon prepared mustard
Nonstick vegetable cooking spray

1. Preheat oven to 350°.
2. In small bowl, combine dry seasonings. Mix well, reserving ½ teaspoon. Sprinkle remaining dry seasoning on chicken and set aside.
3. In shallow baking dish, combine arrowroot, cornmeal, and remainder of dry seasoning. Mix well and set aside.
4. In medium bowl, combine buttermilk, Worcestershire, and mustard. Add chicken, coating well.
5. Dredge chicken in arrowroot mixture and arrange on a large, sprayed baking sheet. Spray each piece of chicken with cooking spray.
6. Bake 30–40 minutes or until golden brown and crispy.

Serves 6

Calories per serving 331
Cholesterol, mg 129
Calories from fat, % 18
Sodium, mg 197

CARIBBEAN "JERK"

"Jerk"—the secret spices of the Caribbean. Serve with steamed rice and an ice-cold beer.

For Jerk seasoning:
  3 tablespoons onion, chopped
  2 tablespoons dried thyme
  2 tablespoons sugar
  3 teaspoons spice blend (or to taste)
  3 teaspoons ground nutmeg
  3 teaspoons freshly ground pepper
  Hot sauce to taste

  1½ pounds boneless, skinless chicken pieces
  1½ tablespoons canola oil

1. To make seasoning, combine all ingredients.
2. To prepare chicken, remove all visible fat and poke several holes in the meat with a fork.
3. Spoon seasoning over both sides of chicken, marinate for at least 20 minutes.
4. In a skillet, heat the oil on medium.
5. Add chicken and cook 5–10 minutes or each side or until fork tender.
6. Serve hot or at room temperature.

Serves 6
Calories per serving 205
Cholesterol, mg 81.7
Calories from fat, % 21
Sodium, mg 92.8

A diet-clobbering dish? No way. Just look at the numbers. You deserve a champagne meal once in a while anyway. Serve with a simple salad.

CHAMPAGNE

4-pound chicken cut into 8 to 10 pieces
8 ounces fresh orange juice
½ tablespoon unsalted butter, melted
16 ounces champagne

1. Preheat oven to 350°.
2. Mix melted butter, orange juice, and champagne in a non-reactive bowl.
3. Add chicken pieces and marinate several hours, or overnight in the refrigerator for more intense flavor.
4. Place chicken in oven and bake about an hour, basting frequently.

Serves 6

Calories per serving 323
Cholesterol, mg 111
Calories from fat, % 9
Sodium, mg 189

CHETTINAD FRIED CHICKEN
(SOUTHERN INDIA)

*2 pounds chicken breasts, skinless, each cut into
    8–10 pieces*
1 teaspoon spice blend
¼ teaspoon ground turmeric
2 tablespoons vegetable oil
½ teaspoon black mustard seeds*
½ teaspoon whole fennel seeds
5 whole dried red chilies (or to taste)
1 medium onion, peeled and chopped
3 tablespoons water

1. Rub ¾-teaspoon. spice blend and the turmeric onto the chicken and set aside for 15 minutes.
2. Add the remaining spice blend in a bowl with water and set aside.
3. Heat the oil in a wok or frying pan over a medium high flame. When hot add the mustard seeds.
4. As soon as this turns red, put in the fennel seeds and red chilies. When they start to darken add the onion and stir fry until it browns lightly.
5. Add the chicken pieces and stir-fry about 5 minutes.
6. Sprinkle a little spiced water at a time from the bowl over the chicken and keep stirring and frying over a medium high flame.
7. Fry the chicken about 10–15 minutes. All the spiced water should be used up.
8. When the chicken is cooked through and slightly browned, remove with a slotted spoon and serve.

A world apart from that of the north. Here's a healthy, though fried, example. Serve with basmati rice and a choice of chutneys.

Serves 4
Calories per serving 325
Cholesterol, mg 131
Calories from fat, % 18
Sodium, mg 150

* Available in Indian markets.

A south-of-the-border favorite that's simple to prepare and even easier to enjoy. Serve with white rice cooked with lime zest.

CILANTRO LIME

4 chicken breasts, boneless, skinless (6 ounces each)
2 teaspoons light soy sauce
2 teaspoons grainy mustard
3 tablespoons fresh lime juice
3 tablespoons minced fresh cilantro leaves
1½ teaspoons sesame oil
1 tablespoon olive oil
½ teaspoon ground cumin
¼ teaspoon crushed red pepper flakes

1. Whisk together soy, mustard, lime juice, cilantro, sesame oil, olive oil, cumin, and red pepper flakes.
2. Place chicken in glass pan, add mixture, and turn to coat evenly.
3. Marinate at room temperature 1 hour, or longer in the refrigerator.
4. Heat a nonstick skillet to medium heat.
5. Remove chicken from marinade and sauté 8–10 minutes on each side or until chicken is cooked through.

Serves 4
Calories per serving 238
Cholesterol, mg 98
Calories from fat, % 29
Sodium, mg 144

CITRUS GRILLED

4 chicken breasts, skinless (4–6 ounces each)
½ teaspoon paprika
2 limes
Spice blend to taste
1 tablespoon olive oil
1½ teaspoon granulated sugar
¼ cup lime juice
½ pint fresh strawberries
½ teaspoon cracked black pepper
½ cup orange sections
½ teaspoon dry mustard

Talk about a perfect summer meal. Serve with a crunchy green salad adorned with orange, apple, and pear slices.

1. Rinse the chicken breasts, pat dry, and place in a shallow dish.
2. Squeeze the juice of the limes over the chicken. Cover, refrigerate at least 4 hours (the longer the better).
3. Preheat the barbecue—it is ready when all the coals have a thick, even coating of gray ash.
4. Blend the oil, lime juice, cracked pepper, dry mustard, paprika, spice blend, and sugar in a small bowl. Set aside.
5. Grill the chicken, basting with the lime juice dressing, until the juices run clear when pierced with a fork (about 10 minutes per side). Add some orange sections to the chicken while grilling.
6. Wash and quarter the strawberries. Drizzle dressing over the chicken.
7. Garnish with orange sections and strawberries.

Serves 4
Calories per serving 237
Cholesterol, mg 82.2
Calories from fat, % 26
Sodium, mg 92.9

A staple in the South for generations. Serve with mashed potatoes and a nice salad.

CORNMEAL CRUSTED

4 chicken breasts, boneless, skinless (4–6 ounces each)
4 tablespoons yellow cornmeal
2 tablespoons chili powder
2 teaspoons ground cumin
2 teaspoons dried oregano
1 teaspoon ground coriander
1 tablespoon canola oil

1. Combine all ingredients, except oil, in large plastic food bag. Add chicken, toss to coat well.
2. Heat oil in nonstick skillet over medium heat.
3. Add chicken. Cook 7 minutes, turn, and cook an additional 7–10 minutes or until cooked through.

Cumin

Serves 4

Calories per serving 306
Cholesterol, mg 120
Calories from fat, % 28
Sodium, mg 146

CROCK-POT ROASTED

2 pounds chicken breasts, skinless, boneless
2 cups chicken broth
3 cups potatoes
1 cup onions, chopped
1 cup celery, sliced
1 cup carrots, sliced thinly
1 teaspoon sweet paprika
½ teaspoon freshly ground black pepper
½ teaspoon sage
½ teaspoon dried thyme
6 oz can no-salt-added tomato paste
¼ cup cold water
3 tablespoons arrowroot

1. Cut chicken pieces into 1" cubes.
2. Peel potatoes and cut into 1" cubes
3. Add the first 11 ingredients to the Crock-Pot.
4. Cover and cook on high 4 hours.
5. Mix water and arrowroot until smooth. Stir into stew.
6. Cook, covered, 30 minutes more or until the vegetables are tender.

Can anything be easier? If you don't have a Crock-Pot... don't make this recipe. So go out and buy one... then make it. You'll have more fun than you can deal with!

Serves 4 to 6

Calories per serving 343
Cholesterol, mg 87.6
Calories from fat, % 7
Sodium, mg 155

Hola! "Havana nice meal like this!" It'll be great with black beans and white rice.

CUBAN

3-pound chicken cut into 8 pieces
6 to 8 cloves garlic, pressed
½ teaspoon ground cumin
¼ cup fresh orange juice
⅛ cup each fresh lemon and lime juice
2 tablespoons olive oil (Spanish if possible)
½ cup dry sherry
1 large onion thinly sliced
8 ounces chicken stock
1 tablespoon arrowroot (optional)
2 tablespoons fresh parsley, finely chopped

1. Wash chicken, pat dry with paper towels.
2. Season chicken liberally with spice blend and pepper. Combine garlic with cumin, and lots of freshly ground black pepper, and rub on and inside chicken.
3. Place chicken in non-reactive bowl and pour orange, lemon and lime juice over it. Cover and refrigerate at least 1 hour or overnight. Remove chicken, reserving marinade, and pat dry.
4. In a heavy bottomed casserole, heat oil over medium heat until fragrant. Brown chicken pieces on all sides.
5. Add reserved marinade, sherry, onion, and chicken stock.
6. Reduce heat to low and simmer until chicken is fork tender, about 35–45 minutes. Transfer chicken to a serving platter, and strain sauce through cheesecloth.
7. Return sauce (with or without arrowroot) to casserole.
8. Cook sauce over low heat until thickened.

Serves 6
Calories per serving 310
Cholesterol, mg 128
Calories from fat, % 29
Sodium, mg 149

DEL MONACO DEVILED

3-pound chicken, cut into 8 pieces
1 teaspoon Dijon-style mustard
½ teaspoon paprika
3 ounces homemade bread crumbs
1 teaspoon red wine vinegar

1. Preheat broiler.
2. Season chicken with spice blend and pepper.
3. Broil 6–8" from flame 15–20 minutes.
4. Meanwhile, blend mustard, paprika, and vinegar in a bowl.
. Place chicken in baking dish, brush with blended ingredients, sprinkle bread crumbs on top.
6. Bake 15–20 minutes.

A devilishy classic offering made heart healthy fer ya! Serve with a fresh spinach and mushroom salad.

Serves 4
Calories per serving 132
Cholesterol, mg 68
Calories from fat, %, . . .11
Sodium, mg 90.5

The name sounds worse than it is unless you're a John Wayne fan. Serve with Spanish rice and a salad.

DIABLO

6 chicken breasts, skinned (4–6 ounces each)
1 tablespoon unsalted butter, melted
1 tablespoon onion, chopped
1 clove garlic, pressed
½ teaspoon basil
½ teaspoon thyme
Spice blend, pepper to taste
⅓ cup plain, low-fat yogurt
⅓ cup no-fat mayonnaise
1 tablespoon coarse mustard

1. Preheat oven to 350°.
2. Place chicken breasts on pieces of foil large enough to wrap each breast individually.
3. Combine the next 6 ingredients and brush on chicken.
4. Seal foil and bake 40 minutes, or until fork tender.
5. Combine yogurt, mayonnaise, and mustard.
6. Spoon mixture over cooked chicken.

Serves 6

Calories per serving 132
Cholesterol, mg 68
Calories from fat, % 11
Sodium, mg 90.5

Basil

DR. ANNE'S CURRY

2 pounds chicken breasts, skinless, boneless, cut into pieces
2 tablespoons canola oil
2 cloves garlic
1 onion
2 to 3 tablespoons roasted black curry powder (available in Middle Eastern grocery stores)
2 tablespoons fresh lime juice
Spice blend
¼ to ½ teaspoon nutmeg
2 ounces 2% evaporated milk
½ ounce dried, unsweetened, shredded coconut

1. Cut the chicken into small pieces.
2. Dice the onions and garlic.
3. Mix onion, garlic, spices, lime juice, and spice blend. Cover chicken and marinate for two to three hours (or overnight for more taste), refrigerated.
4. Place the chicken in a nonstick skillet, on a very low fire, and heat about 10 minutes, turning occasionally. Raise heat to medium. Cook another 20 minutes.
5. 5 minutes before serving, add the shredded coconut and evaporated milk, stirring gently.

I'm naming this one in honor of my favorite Diabetologist. She's the "sweet" one with the fiery taste buds and "riata-like" persona. Serve with basmati rice and chutney.

Serves 6
Calories per serving 245
Cholesterol, mg 88.4
Calories from fat, % 29
Sodium, mg 113

Here's a real easy one, with great color, especially if served with a pea, carrot and corn medley of steamed veggies, or even over pasta.

EGGPLANT AND ROASTED RED PEPPER SAUCE

4 *chicken breasts, boneless and skinless (4-6 ounces each)*
2 *red bell peppers*
2 *small Chinese or Italian eggplants*
3 *tablespoons olive oil*
1 *onion, sliced*
2 *garlic cloves, chopped*
¼ *cup red wine vinegar*

To Roast Peppers
   Place the peppers on the grill, over the burner, or under the broiler, turning them, until charred all over, nearly black. Remove and place in a brown paper bag to steam off skin. When cool enough to handle, remove charred skin and seed them.

1. Preheat the grill or broiler.
2. Halve the eggplant, score in 2 or 3 places, and brush with some of the oil.
3. Place on the grill, cut side toward the heat. Turn after 5 minutes.
4. Cook until almost soft.
5. Add the chicken breasts and cook 3 minutes on each side, until done. Remove to a plate.
6. Heat the remaining oil in a large frying pan until it begins to smoke.
7. Lower heat, add the onion and garlic, and cook until soft.
8. Puree the peppers and vinegar in a food processor or blender until smooth.
9. Add the puree, eggplants, and chicken to the frying pan, and heat together, about 5 minutes.
10. Place the chicken mixture on a platter surrounded by the eggplant and sauce. Sprinkle with the herbs.

Serves 4

Calories per serving 259
Cholesterol, mg 82.2
Calories from fat, % 30
Sodium, mg 95.7

EGYPTIAN

1½ pounds chicken breasts, skinless, boneless
5 cloves garlic, crushed
Juice of 2 lemons
1 tablespoon olive oil

1. Combine the crushed garlic and 1 tablespoon of lemon juice. Rub a small amount of this mixture on the chicken pieces.
2. Prepare a marinade of olive oil and the remaining lemon juice. Pour it over the chicken pieces and marinate for at least 1 hour. (Overnight is preferable)
3. Cook over hot coals or under the broiler until both sides are done.
4. Baste with the remaining garlic and lemon marinade.

If your "mummy" didn't make this one for you, she should have! This is wonderful with roasted eggplant and salad.

Serves 6
Calories per serving 152
Cholesterol, mg 65.7
Calories from fat, % 23
Sodium, mg 74.3

ETHIOPIAN WOT

This is a recipe for a very hot (toasty, spicy) stewlike dish. Serve with lots of pita or better yet, Ethiopian bread (injera). This freezes well for future use.

1 pound chicken breasts, skinless, boneless
½ pound chicken thighs, skinless, boneless
Juice of 2 lemons
3 pounds onions, very finely chopped
1 pound of garlic, mashed
¼ pound mashed ginger
2 tablespoons Ethiopian chili powder (bere bere)
or cayenne pepper
1 tablespoon unsalted butter
Pinch of spice blend, pepper to taste, nutmeg, or cumin
(optional)
1 hard-boiled egg per person

1. Wash chicken well, let stand in spice-blended and lemoned water.
2. Cook onion over low heat, without any fat, stirring constantly until all juices have evaporated and onions are slightly browned. Add the butter; cook 15–20 minutes over low heat.
3. Add 1 tablespoon of hot water occasionally until mixture is slightly pasty. Add chili powder. If it looks too dry, add hot water and stir. Cook 30–45 minutes, stirring frequently, adding hot water if necessary. Do not let it brown—the chili powder will become bitter. Add garlic and ginger. Simmer 15 minutes. Add water as needed.
4. Remove chicken, squeezing each piece to remove as much water as possible. Cut small slits in the meat to allow sauce to penetrate. Cook the meat in sauce (uncovered) until tender, about 30 minutes, stirring occasionally.
5. Add spices to taste just before removing from stove.
6. Add 1 sliced hard-boiled egg per person.

Serves 6
Calories per serving 440
Cholesterol, mg 184
Calories from fat, % 22
Sodium, mg 139

FIG STUFFED

4 chicken breasts, boneless, skinless (4–6 ounces each)
2 tablespoons unsalted butter
1 scallion (green onion)
2 ounces mushrooms
1 slice white bread
½ ounce blue cheese
1 ounce dried figs
Spice blend and freshly ground black pepper to taste

1. Preheat the oven to 375°.
2. Butter a medium baking dish.
3. Melt the remaining butter in a skillet.
4. Slice the scallions diagonally, add to the butter, and allow to soften over low heat.
5. Trim and wipe the mushrooms and cut them each into 2 or 3 pieces. Chop them in a food processor and add to the scallions with some spice blend and pepper. Let cook over high heat 2 to 3 minutes, until their liquid evaporates.
6. Process the bread into crumbs
7. Crumble the blue cheese and chop the figs.
8. When the mushrooms are fairly dry, take the pan from the heat and stir in the breadcrumbs, cheese, and figs.
9. Cut a pocket into each breast about 3" long and 1" deep. Fill with the stuffing and set the breasts in the buttered dish.
10. Cover with foil and bake in the heated oven 30 to 35 minutes or until no pink juice runs out when you cut into the center of the biggest breast with a knife.

I know, I know, it sounds awful. Just give yourself the chance to enjoy the many levels of taste in this one. C'mon! Serve it with mashed potatoes and a green salad.

Serves 4

Calories per serving 209
Cholesterol, mg 78.4
Calories from fat, % 28
Sodium, mg 163

Another classic Italian meal made heart healthy. Serve with any kind of pasta.

FLORENTINE

6 chicken breasts, skinless (4 ounces each)
1 bunch fresh spinach, chopped
4 ounces whole-milk ricotta cheese
4 ounces mushrooms, finely chopped
½ cup chopped fresh chives or green onion tops
2 tablespoons Chinese mustard

1. Preheat oven to 450°.
2. Melt butter in heavy skillet over medium heat. Add mushrooms and sauté until tender, about 5 minutes. Cool slightly.
3. Blend spinach, ricotta cheese, and chives in medium bowl. Mix in mushrooms; season with spice blend and pepper.
4. Place chicken between two sheets of wax paper and pound to ¼" thickness, fill with spinach mixture, roll up and tie with string.
5. Arrange chicken breasts on baking sheet and spread mustard evenly over each piece.
6. Bake 20–25 minutes.

Serves 6

Calories per serving 211
Cholesterol, mg 81.4
Calories from fat, % 29
Sodium, mg 151

40 BAY LEAF

16 ounces chicken breasts, skinless, boneless
8 ounces chicken thigh, skinless, boneless
2 teaspoons olive oil
Juice of one lemon
2 teaspoons unsalted butter
40 bay leaves
5 cloves garlic, crushed
½ cup flour
Spice blend and freshly ground black pepper
2 tablespoons heavy cream
2 tablespoons brandy or grappa (optional)

1. Preheat oven to 300°.
2. Heat the oil and butter in a large skillet.
3. Add the bay leaves and garlic and fry over moderate heat about 5 minutes or until crisp.
4. Season the flour with spice blend and pepper for coating the chicken parts.
5. Push the bay leaves and garlic to one side and fry the chicken in the same pan over moderate heat about 10 minutes or until evenly browned. Transfer the chicken, bay leaves, and juices to an ovenproof casserole.
6. Cover and bake 1 hour and 15 minutes. Remove the chicken and keep warm.
7. Stir the cream and the lemon juice into the casserole and reheat over low heat. Do not boil or remove the bay leaves.
8. Pour sauce and bay leaves over the chicken.

Note: Heat the brandy or *grappa* in a ladle or tablespoon over a naked flame until it ignites, and pour it over the chicken before serving.

A dish for anyone with a flourishing laurel (bay) tree who can never think of enough uses for the leaves. If you don't have a laurel tree, dried bay leaves will also give good results. Serve with mashed potatoes and a tomato salad.

Serves 4

Cholesterol, mg 85
Calories per serving 269
Calories from fat, % 30
Sodium, mg 85.6

Mozambique, a one-time Portuguese colony in the east of Africa, maintains its culinary heritage with garlic and ginger. Serve with individual bowls of steamed rice and cold beer.

FRANGO A CAFRIAL
(MOZAMBIQUE)

2 pounds chicken breasts, skinless, boneless
1 teaspoon cayenne pepper (or to taste)
1 teaspoon garlic, minced
½ teaspoon ginger, minced
1 teaspoon paprika
1 ounce canola oil

1. Combine all spices in oil and mix thoroughly.
2. Rub chicken with the seasoned oil on all sides.
3. Roast, broil, or barbecue the chicken in your favorite manner, basting it from time to time with the seasoned oil until done. (If roasting, use whole chicken and roast in a 400° oven 30 minutes, then lower heat to 350° and finish roasting an additional 45 minutes. Percentage of calories from fat will exceed 30%.)
4. Serve with plenty of white rice (allow 1 cup cooked rice per person).

Serves 6

Calories per serving 210
Cholesterol, mg 87.6
Calories from fat, % 30
Sodium, mg 98.6

FRAREJ
(LEBANON)

4 chicken breasts with skins and ribs (4–6 ounces each)
½ teaspoon spice blend
Juice of 3 large lemons
2 tablespoons olive oil
2 large potatoes, skinned, cut into ½" cubes
2 minced garlic cloves
4 or more roma tomatoes
1 large white onion, sliced into half-circles
lemon/olive oil mixture

1. Preheat the oven to 500°.
2. Rinse the chicken breasts in cold water. Rub with spice blend.
3. Place the potatoes into a 9"x13" baking dish. Stir lemon juice, olive oil, garlic, and coat the potatoes. Bake in oven 10 minutes.
4. Add the chicken breasts and tomatoes to the baking dish. Generously spoon the hot lemon/oil/garlic mixture over the chicken. Return dish to oven and cook uncovered 20 minutes, or until the chicken skins turn dark brown, meat is firm, and doesn't ooze when poked with a fork.
5. Baste the chicken breasts two or three times with lemon/oil mixture during cooking.
6. Remove skin and serve.

For those of you who don't speak Lebanese—I dare you to try to pronounce this one! Another Middle Eastern winner and great, as is, with warmed pita bread.

Serves 4
Calories per serving 231
Cholesterol, mg 65.3
Calories from fat, % 24
Sodium, mg 82.4

A great barbecue recipe...lots of spice, but not too hot. Add corn on the cob and a salad, and you've got it all!

GARLIC AND CORIANDER

1 pound chicken breasts, skinless, boneless
8 ounces thighs, skinless and boneless
7 cloves garlic
8 ounces fresh coriander
2 tablespoons lemon juice

1. Put garlic in a food processor on medium speed. Gradually add the coriander, then lemon juice, mixing until a paste is formed.
2. Coat the chicken pieces with the paste. Marinate at least 2 hours at room temperature or refrigerate overnight.
3. Grill 7–9 minutes or until crisp.

Serves 6
Calories per serving 177
Cholesterol, mg 79.7
Calories from fat, % 28
Sodium, mg 93.7

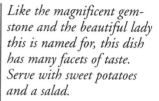

GARNET

1½ pounds chicken breasts, skinless, boneless
¾ cup sugar
⅓ cup arrowroot
¼ cup chopped onion
Spice blend and freshly ground pepper to taste
¾ cup orange juice
2 teaspoons unsalted butter
¼ teaspoon cinnamon
1½ cups fresh cranberries or 1 small can whole jellied
cranberries (omit the sugar if you're using the canned
*   cranberries)*
¼ teaspoon ginger

1. Coat chicken in arrowroot/spice blend mixture.
2. Brown 5 minutes per side in melted butter.
3. Combine remaining ingredients in saucepan. Bring to a
   boil. Pour over chicken.
4. Cover and cook slowly 35–40 minutes.

Like the magnificent gemstone and the beautiful lady this is named for, this dish has many facets of taste. Serve with sweet potatoes and a salad.

Serves 6
Calories per serving 400
Cholesterol, mg 69.2
Calories from fat, % 6
Sodium, mg 96.8

This is what a summer-y kinda BBQ is all about! Serve with a crisp salad and grilled veggies.

GIN AND LEMON GRILLED

4 whole chicken breasts, skinless boneless 4-6 ounces each
¼ cup fresh lemon juice
1 teaspoon lemon rind
¼ cup gin
2 teaspoons chopped fresh oregano or ½ teaspoon dried oregano
Spice blend and freshly ground black pepper to taste
1 teaspoon sugar
2 ounces canola oil

1. In a shallow dish whisk together the lemon juice, the gin, the oregano, the salt, the spice blend, and pepper to taste.
2. Add the oil in a stream, and whisk the marinade until it is emulsified.
3. Add the chicken, coating it well with the marinade, and allow it to marinate, covered and chilled, 20 minutes.
4. Grill the chicken on an oiled rack set about 6 inches over glowing coals, 7 minutes on each side, or until it is cooked through.

Serves 6

Calories per serving 133
Cholesterol, mg 43.8
Calories from fat, % 22
Sodium, mg 49.5

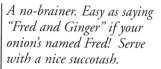

GINGER AND ONION

1½ pounds chicken breasts, skinless, boneless
6 large yellow onions, sliced about ⅛" thick
1½ tablespoons ground ginger
1½ teaspoons freshly ground pepper
1 cup water
Chopped parsley for garnish

1. Place half of onion slices in bottom of Dutch oven or any large heavy-bottomed pot with lid.
2. Mix ginger and pepper, and spread out over a piece of wax paper. Roll each piece of chicken in ginger mixture, making sure to shake off any excess seasoning.
3. Place chicken pieces in pot on top of onions and cover with remaining onion slices. Cover with water and a lid.
4. Braise over medium low heat 2 hours.
5. Serve in bowls and garnish with chopped parsley.

A no-brainer. Easy as saying "Fred and Ginger" if your onion's named Fred! Serve with a nice succotash.

Serves 6
Calories per serving 140
Cholesterol, mg 65.7
Calories from fat, % 10
Sodium, mg 75

One of a million culinary gifts from China. Serve with million-year-old rice. or a thousand-year-old egg if you can find one.

GINGER SESAME

1 pound chicken breasts, boneless and skinless
1 tablespoon canola oil
2 tablespoons honey
1 tablespoon paprika
½ teaspoon cinnamon
1¼ teaspoon ground ginger
¼ teaspoon ground black pepper
1 tablespoon sesame seeds

1. Preheat grill.
2. In a cup, combine oil and honey. Set aside.
3. In another cup, combine paprika, ginger, cinnamon, and pepper.
4. Using a fork, pierce chicken pieces. Rub spice mixture on both sides of chicken.
5. Cook 2–3" from coals until chicken is nearly done, about 3 minutes on each side.
6. Brush with reserved honey mixture. Sprinkle with sesame seeds.
7. Grill another minute.

Serves 4

Calories per serving 206
Cholesterol, mg 65.7
Calories from fat, % 27
Sodium, mg 75

GREEK ROASTED

3 pound chicken, cut into 8 pieces
1 cup onion, chopped
1 teaspoon each oregano and mint
¼ teaspoon each cinnamon and nutmeg
Juice of 1 lemon
Pinch of cayenne pepper
1 tablespoon olive oil
Paprika

1. Preheat oven to 375°.
2. Wash the chicken thoroughly and place pieces in a bowl just large enough to hold them.
3. Combine remaining ingredients in a small bowl, then pour the mixture over the chicken pieces.
4. Cover the chicken and marinate in this mixture at least 3 hours, preferably overnight, shifting the pieces to make sure they're all benefiting from the marinade.
5. Place the chicken pieces in a shallow baking dish, pour the marinade over them, and sprinkle with paprika. Bake uncovered in the oven about an hour and 20 minutes, basting frequently.

Every Greek family eats this dish, just as they have been for hundreds of years. Serve with a nice cucumber salad and pita bread.

Serves 4–6
Calories per serving 303
Cholesterol, mg 159
Calories from fat, % 29
Sodium, mg 177

*Relax, the sauce is green,
not the chicken!
Serve with pasta and a salad*

GREEN WITH PUMPKIN SEEDS

*1½ pounds chicken breasts, skinless, boneless
1 tablespoon olive oil
1 tablespoon butter
1 large onion, finely chopped
1 garlic clove chopped
1 cup chicken stock
1 cup dry white wine
1 cup roasted pumpkin seeds
1 10-ounce can Mexican green tomatoes, drained
½ cup chopped parsley*

1. In a large skillet, sauté chicken in heated olive oil and butter until golden.
2. Transfer chicken to ovenproof casserole and cover.
3. Sauté onion and garlic until limp and golden. Add to chicken with wine. Cook over very low heat until chicken is tender, about 7–10 minutes.
4. Put pumpkin seeds in a blender or food processor. Add green tomatoes and parsley. Process a few more seconds.
5. Add mixture to casserole, simmering gently 5 minutes, until sauce has thickened to a medium consistency.

Serves 6

Calories per serving 262
Cholesterol, mg 70.9
Calories from fat, % 27
Sodium, mg 94.9

GUATAMALAN

1 pound chicken breasts, boneless, skinless
1 tablespoon peanut oil
2 onions, diced
4 cloves garlic
4 tomatoes, roasted, chopped
4 Pablano chilies (or to taste)
1 teaspoon oregano
1 teaspoon thyme
1½ cups chicken stock

1. Dice chicken into 1" cubes.
2. In 1 tablespoon of heated oil, sauté chicken over medium heat until lightly browned.
3. Remove chicken, and add vegetables to the same pan. Heat until tender.
4. Remove vegetables and puree until smooth.
5. Return to pan.
6. Add chicken, and simmer over low heat 20 minutes; serve.

Guatemalans are so proud of their country's name that they named their capital after it! Serve with rice and a corn salad.

Serves 4
Calories per serving 194
Cholesterol, mg 65.3
Calories from fat, % 24
Sodium, mg 81

Why shucks…this li'l ol'
recipe jest screams
for mashed tater 'n' peas.

HONEY-MINT ROASTED

4-pound roasting chicken
Spice blend, freshly ground pepper to taste
½ teaspoon paprika
¼ cup honey
2 tablespoons lemon juice
1 tablespoon unsalted butter
2 teaspoons mint jelly
1 teaspoon grated lemon zest

1. Preheat oven to 350°.
2. Place chicken in roasting pan. Rub spice blend, pepper and paprika in cavity of bird.
3. Roast 1 hour.
4. In saucepan, mix honey, lemon juice, unsalted butter, mint jelly, and lemon zest, stirring constantly until unsalted butter and jelly melt.
5. Brush chicken with sauce and roast another 20 minutes.

Serves 6

Calories per serving 316
Cholesterol, mg   137
Calories from fat, % 30
Sodium, mg 121

Mint

HORSERADISH BAKED

6 chicken breasts, skin removed, about 4 ounces each
½ cup white wine
1 tablespoon vegetable oil
¼ cup freshly grated horseradish
1¼ teaspoons mustard seeds
½ teaspoon onion powder
½ teaspoon garlic powder
¼ teaspoon dried thyme
2 tablespoons fresh parsley, chopped finely

1. Preheat oven to 350°.
2. Pour wine into casserole dish; add chicken breasts.
3. Using pastry brush, baste each piece of chicken with the oil.
4. Spread grated horseradish equally on each breast.
5. Bake, covered, about 30 minutes.
6. While chicken is baking, grind mustard seed and combine with remaining ingredients.
7. After 30 minutes, baste chicken with the wine sauce in the pan.
8. Pour mustard seed mixture over chicken and bake, uncovered, another 20 to 30 minutes, until chicken is tender.

A lusty flavored dish that's perfect with spinach and mashed potatoes.

Horseradish

Serves 6

Calories per serving 167
Cholesterol, mg 65.7
Calories from fat, % 21
Sodium, mg 84.5

What does a Scotsman keep under his kilt? Maybe it's this simple recipe! Serve with sautéed leeks and a nice salad.

HOWTOWDIE
(SCOTTISH)

OAT STUFFING

1 large onion, finely chopped
2 ounces unsalted butter
1 cup regular rolled oats
1 teaspoon spice blend
½ teaspoon ground coriander
½ teaspoon freshly ground pepper
⅛ teaspoon grated nutmeg

6 chicken breasts, skinless, boneless (4–6 ounces each)
6 medium onions
2 ounces unsalted butter, melted

1. Preheat oven to 375°.
2. Cook and stir onion in butter in 10" skillet over medium heat until light brown. Stir in remaining ingredients.
3. Cook and stir until oats are golden brown and crisp, about 3 to 4 minutes.
4. Cut a pocket in each breast about 3" long and 1" deep. Fill pocket with stuffing mixture.
5. Place chicken in shallow casserole.
6. Cut onions in half and arrange around the chicken.
7. Brush chicken and onions with melted butter.
8. Roast uncovered in oven, brushing chicken and onions several times with remaining butter until chicken and onions are done, about 1½ hours.

Serves 6
Calories per serving 330
Cholesterol, mg   108
Calories from fat, % 29
Sodium, mg 130

HUNGARIAN PAPRIKAS

2 pounds chicken breasts, skinless, cut into 8 pieces
2 large onions
6 medium-sized potatoes (cut into 4 pieces)
1 level tablespoon of sweet Hungarian paprika
2 tablespoons of Spanish olive oil
1 tablespoon low-sodium tomato paste
Spice blend to taste

1. Place oil in large skillet, add finely chopped onions, and simmer till soft and brown.
2. Add chicken pieces. Continue to simmer a few minutes, then add water till meats are covered.
3. Cook on medium until boiling, add potatoes, and cook till potatoes are about two-thirds done.
4. Add tomato paste and sweet paprika, and cook till potatoes are done.
5. Add spice blend to taste and cook another few minutes.
6. Remove from stove let it sit for 15–20 minutes, and serve.

What would a classic Hungarian dish be without that flavorable, fragrant Hungarian paprika ? All answers become the property of the author! Serve this over the classic buttered and parsleyed noodles.

Serves 4
Calories per serving 435
Cholesterol, mg 131
Calories from fat, % 21
Sodium, mg 158

IMOYO
(NIGERIAN)

"Imoyo" is the name given dishes of this type by slaves liberated from Brazil who settled in Lagos. Very often, onions, peppers, and tomatoes are not cooked but added raw at the last moment. The choice is yours. Serve with rice and yams.

1½ pounds chicken breasts, skinless, boneless
10 ounces chicken thighs, skinless, boneless
2 teaspoons spice blend
Freshly ground black pepper to taste
¼ teaspoon crushed red pepper flakes
2 medium onions, peeled and cut into quarters
2 quarts chicken stock
4 tomatoes
1 pound fresh okra (ends cut and left whole; or use one 16-ounce can okra, drained)
4 green bell peppers, seeded and cut into quarters
1 teaspoon chili powder (or to taste)
4 tablespoons tomato paste
2 tablespoons freshly squeezed lemon or lime juice
2 tablespoons unsalted butter

1. Place first six ingredients in a 4-quart saucepan:
2. Add chicken stock.
3. Simmer gently 30 minutes.
4. Add tomatoes, fresh okra, bell peppers, chili powder, tomato paste, and lemon or lime juice.
5. Simmer until vegetables and chicken are cooked.
6. Check the seasoning and add spice blend and more pepper if needed
7. Drain vegetables and chicken from the stock and place in serving bowl.
8. Add butter and allow it to melt over chicken and vegetables. Use the stock for cooking rice or yams.

Serves 8
Calories per serving 247
Cholesterol, mg 90.7
Calories from fat, % 30
Sodium, mg 100

INDONESIAN KABOBS

3 pounds chicken breasts, boneless and skinless
¼ cup shallots, minced
1 teaspoon ginger
1 tablespoon garlic
1 teaspoon coriander
3 tablespoons brown sugar
2 tablespoons fresh lemon juice
2 tablespoons non-fat evaporated milk

1. In a bowl, combine all ingredients. Add chicken.
2. Marinate in refrigerator overnight.
3. Thread pieces on skewers and grill until tender.

Indonesian food is one of the spiciest in the world...but here's a mild one.
As with all food from this part of the world, basmati rice works wonders.

Serves 6 to 8
Calories per serving 210
Cholesterol, mg 99.2
Calories from fat, % 10
Sodium, mg 117

This one's from the beautiful island of Barbados. They have a spice mix there called "bajan". The original calls for all sorts of really hot chilies. If it makes you happy, use 'em, but don't blame me if your tongue catches fire and gets in front of your eyeteeth, and you can't see what you're saying! Serve with rice and a cooling fruit salad.

ISLAND

(The alternate suggestions in parentheses are what I use...but I'm a wimp!)

6 chicken breasts, skinless, boneless (4–6 ounces each)
3 fresh Habanero chiles, finely chopped (or jalapeños)
1 tablespoon Habanero sauce (or Tabasco)
6 green onions, finely chopped, including tops
3 cloves garlic, minced
2 tablespoons freshly squeezed lime juice
2 tablespoons fresh parsley, chopped (or cilantro)
½ teaspoon ground cinnamon
½ teaspoon freshly ground black pepper
1 egg
1 tablespoon low-sodium soy sauce
Flour for dredging
1 cup uncooked rice
2 tablespoons canola oil

1. Combine the chilies, green onions, garlic, lime juice, parsley, cinnamon, and ground pepper.
2. Cut deep gashes in the chicken and fill with the mixture.
3. Beat the egg and combine with the soy sauce and pepper sauce.
4. Process rice until it's the consistency of flour. Dip chicken in the egg mixture and roll in the rice flour.
5. Heat the oil to 375° and fry the chicken until golden brown, 3–4 minutes on each side.

Serves 6

Calories per serving 309
Cholesterol, mg   101
Calories from fat, % 21
Sodium, mg 189

ISRAELI WITH NECTARINES

1 pound chicken breasts, skinless
10 ounces chicken thighs, skinless
½ cup orange juice
2 tablespoons lemon juice
¼ cup honey
2 to 4 seeded and finely chopped chili peppers
4 nectarines, thinly sliced

1. Preheat oven to 350°.
2. Combine orange juice, lemon juice, and honey.
3. Pour mixture over chicken pieces and sprinkle with chili peppers.
4. Bake, covered in foil, 45 minutes, basting with pan juices frequently to ensure moistness.
5. Add nectarines. Bake an additional 5 minutes or until nectarines are heated throughout.
6. Remove foil and bake an additional 10 minutes until brown.

A recipe as old as Israel itself…and that's only since 1948!
A fresh fruit salad complements this nicely.

Serves 6
Calories per serving 267
Cholesterol, mg 88.7
Calories from fat, % 22
Sodium, mg 91.6

A delicious recipe with peanut butter, and terrific on top of rice.

JAKARTA
(INDONESIA)

1½ pounds chicken breasts, skinless, boneless
10 ounces chicken stock
2–3 tablespoons low-fat, low-salt, crunchy peanut butter
(don't use smooth—it just isn't the same)
Vegetable spray
3 green onions, chopped
3 tomatoes, seeded and chopped
2 cloves garlic, crushed
Pinch cayenne pepper or to taste

1. Heat oven to 350°.
2. Spray a shallow baking dish, and place chicken in it.
3. Mix together the remaining ingredients and pour over the chicken.
4. Bake until chicken is cooked and sauce is bubbling, about 40 minutes.
5. Baste once or twice during the baking.

Serves 6

Calories per serving 185
Cholesterol, mg 65.7
Calories from fat, % 25
Sodium, mg 107

JAPANESE

1½ pounds chicken breasts, boneless, skinless, and diced
2 teaspoons low-sodium soy sauce
⅛ cup sugar
Fresh ginger and garlic to taste
3 tablespoons sake (Japanese rice wine)
1 tablespoon canola oil

1. In a mixing bowl, combine all ingredients except the oil.
2. Add chicken and marinate for at least an hour.
3. Heat oil in a nonstick skillet or wok.
4. Add the chicken with marinade.
5. Cover and simmer 30 minutes.

You'll bow with respect to this offering!
Serve with a cooling cucumber salad and Japanese-style rice.

Serves 4
Calories per serving 294
Cholesterol, mg 98.6
Calories from fat, % 17
Sodium, mg 195

She's a friend of mine from Philadelphia. I know, I know—big deal!
Serve with sautéed cherry tomatoes and hot fettuccine.

JESSICA'S

4 chicken breasts, skinless (4 ounces each)
1 tablespoon unsalted butter
2 tablespoons shallots, finely chopped
2 cloves garlic, crushed
1 cup mushrooms, sliced
2 ounces chicken stock
2 tablespoons brandy (optional)
2 tablespoons Dijon mustard
1 tablespoon Worcestershire sauce
2 tablespoons parsley, finely chopped

1. Melt butter in nonstick skillet over medium heat.
2. Add shallots and garlic. Cook 2 minutes. Add mushrooms. Stir and cook additional 3 to 4 minutes. Remove from heat and set aside.
3. Increase heat to medium high. Add chicken breasts and cook 20 to 25 minutes, turning once. Remove to warm platter. Lower heat to medium.
4. Add stock, brandy, mustard, Worcestershire sauce, and mushroom mixture. Bring to a boil.
5. Cook until mixture is slightly reduced—about 2 minutes.
6. Spoon sauce over chicken and sprinkle with parsley.

Serves 4

Calories per serving 188
Cholesterol, mg 76
Calories from fat, % 24
Sodium, mg 170

JORDANIAN LEMON

5–6 pound chicken, skinless , cut into 8–10 serving pieces
2½ cups water
3 cardamon seeds, crushed
1 tablespoon rose water
2 tablespoons lemon juice
½ teaspoon saffron
Spice blend and freshly ground pepper to taste
2 tablespoons arrowroot
½ cup water

1. In a 4-quart pan, combine 2½ cups water, cardamom, rose water, lemon juice, saffron and spice blend.
2. On high heat, bring the mixture to a boil. Reduce heat to medium.
3. Dissolve the arrowroot in the ½-cup water, then add to the liquid slowly with continuous mixing.
4. When mixture thickens, add chicken pieces. Cover and cook until chicken pieces are tender, about 20–25 minutes.

You should be able to find rose water and cardamom seeds at any Middle Eastern market. None around? Use quarter-teaspoon ground cardamom from the spice aisle of your local grocery. Substitute rose water with a good thought!
Serve over rice.

Cardamom

Serves 8

Calories per serving 237
Cholesterol, mg 136
Calories from fat, % 21
Sodium, mg 157

Three kinds of pepper and some kinda kick! This is much better than poi, I promise. Serve over rice with pineapple.

KAUAI THREE PEPPER
(HAWAIIAN)

3 pounds chicken breasts, skinless, boneless
½ cup chicken stock
1 large onion, sliced
1 green bell pepper, cut into strips
1 red bell pepper, cut into strips
2 teaspoons each of coarsely ground pink, green,and black
*   peppercorns*

1. Cut chicken into bite-size pieces.
2. In a wok or skillet, heat 2 tablespoons of stock. Stir-fry chicken.
3. Add onion, bell peppers, and remaining stock. Stir-fry until vegetables are tender.
4. Add peppercorns.

Serves 6

Calories per serving 260
Cholesterol, mg 131
Calories from fat, % 11
Sodium, mg 147

KEY LIME BROILED

4 pounds chicken breasts, skinless
4 ounces fresh lime juice
2 ounces olive oil
1 tablespoon onion, grated
2 teaspoons tarragon, crushed
¼ teaspoon freshly ground black pepper
Vegetable cooking spray

1. Place chicken on a vegetable oil–sprayed rack, in a broiler pan.
2. Mix lime juice, olive oil, onion, tarragon, and pepper in a bowl. Brush generously over chicken.
3. Broil, turning every 10 minutes, basting with remaining lime mixture 40 minutes or until breasts are tender and golden brown. Remove to a heated platter and serve.

The real key to this dish is that it's a lot healthier than it looks and tastes!
Serve with white rice flavored with lime zest.

Serves 6

Calories per serving 315
Cholesterol, mg 131
Calories from fat, % 29
Sodium, mg 146

The Seoul of Oriental cooking. A side dish of spicy kimchi and white rice is perfect with it.

KOREAN

2 pounds chicken breasts, skinless, boneless, cut into pieces
¼ cup apple juice (or sweet wine)
2 teaspoons Japanese-style low-sodium soy sauce
4 to 6 cloves garlic, minced
Pinch red pepper, cayenne or dash hot pepper sauce
4 tablespoons toasted sesame seeds

1. Preheat oven to 375°.
2. Trim all excess fat from chicken and discard.
3. Place chicken pieces in a large plastic bag set inside a bowl.
4. Combine remaining ingredients (except sesame seeds) into a marinade and pour into bag, covering chicken pieces. Close bag tightly. Marinate in refrigerator 2–24 hours.
5. Remove chicken from marinade and arrange on shallow nonstick baking pan.
6. Bake in oven 45 minutes, broil or barbecue until done.
7. Sprinkle with sesame seeds before serving.

Sesame

Serves 6
Calories per serving 211
Cholesterol, mg 87.6
Calories from fat, % 22
Sodium, mg 156

KUWAITI

1½ pounds chicken breasts, skinless
4 tablespoons plain, low-fat yogurt
1 teaspoon turmeric powder
1 cup onion, finely chopped
1 teaspoon powdered ginger
1 teaspoon garlic powder
2 teaspoons chili powder
2 teaspoons coriander powder
2 tablespoons peanut oil
Spice blend to taste

1. Cut chicken into pieces. Marinate with yogurt and spice blend. Set aside one hour.
2. Heat oil and sauté turmeric. Add onion and sauté till light brown.
3. Add ginger and garlic mixed with 1 tablespoon of water. Stir well.
4. Add chili and coriander mixed in 4 tablespoons of water.
5. Add chicken and sufficient water to make a good sauce. Cover and cook on low heat till chicken is done. Cooking takes about half an hour to 45 minutes, depending on size of chicken pieces and level of heat.

This is a multiflavored dish from a low, undulating desert country.
Serve with couscous, the Middle Eastern pasta.

Serves 6

Calories per serving 159
Cholesterol, mg 66.4
Calories from fat, % 23
Sodium, mg 81.5

Another of the Middle East's grand flavor inventions. Put this together with roasted eggplant and rice pilaf.

LEBANESE

5-pound roasting chicken, cut into 8–10 pieces
2 tablespoons canola oil
2 large yellow onions, chopped
2 to 3 cloves garlic, chopped
2 cups plain, low-fat yogurt
½-cup fresh chopped parsley
Sumac (available in Middle Eastern markets)

1. Preheat oven to 375°.
2. Pan brown the chicken pieces in oil.
3. Place chicken in heat-proof baking dish, leaving 1 table-spoon of oil in pan.
4. Add the onions, garlic, and yogurt to the pan, warming through. Pour mixture over chicken pieces. Season with spice blend and pepper. Cover chicken pieces with parsley.
5. Bake in the oven 40–45 minutes.
6. Sprinkle sumac over chicken pieces; serve immediately.

Serves 6
Calories per serving 290
Cholesterol, mg 109
Calories from fat, % 30
Sodium, mg 170

LEMON-HERB ROASTED

2 pounds chicken breasts, boneless, cut into pieces
½ cup chicken stock
2 tablespoons Worcestershire sauce
1 tablespoon fresh lemon juice
1 tablespoon oregano
1 teaspoon marjoram
½ teaspoon thyme
2 cloves minced garlic
2 strips lemon peel, each ½" x 1"
2 tablespoons white wine

1. Preheat oven to 325°.
2. Sprinkle chicken with spice blend and pepper. Arrange in large, shallow baking pan.
3. In a small sauce pan, combine stock, Worcestershire sauce, lemon juice, dry seasonings, garlic, and lemon peel. Bring to a boil.
4. Add wine and spoon over chicken, covering each piece. Let stand about 20 minutes.
5. Bake uncovered 30 minutes. Turn chicken, spoon on more marinade, and bake 30 minutes.

Marjoram

Back in the United States with an easy dish. Marry it with roasted potatoes and a green salad.

Serves 6

Calories per serving 263
Cholesterol, mg 129
Calories from fat, % 20
Sodium, mg 168

The two flavors of this dish are a pleasant surprise when you first try them. Serve with roasted potatoes and a green salad. Add some mint and a lemony vinaigrette dressing.

LEMON MINT

4 chicken breasts, boneless, skinless
Grated peel of 2 lemons
Juice of 2 lemons (about ⅓ cup)
¼ cup mint, finely chopped
¼ cup honey
1 teaspoon olive oil
Pinch of cayenne pepper
½ teaspoon spice blend
Freshly grated black pepper to taste

1. In a mixing bowl, combine lemon juice, peel, mint, honey, olive oil, spice blend, cayenne, and pepper.
2. Pour half the mixture over the chicken and marinate 15 minutes to 1 hour at room temperature (if you want to marinate for a longer time, make sure the chicken and mixture are refrigerated)
3. Remove chicken from marinade.
4. In a heavy nonstick skillet set over medium heat, sauté breasts about 5 minutes on each side. (Chicken can also be grilled on medium coals 5–7 minutes.)
5. Spoon remaining lemon-mint mixture over chicken and serve.

Serves 4
Calories per serving 207
Cholesterol, mg 68
Calories from fat, % 21
Sodium, mg 76.9

LEMON PARSLEY

¾ pound chicken breasts, boneless and skinless
1 tablespoon oil
1½ cups chicken stock
1½ cups instant brown rice
2 tablespoons parsley, chopped
1 teaspoon grated lemon peel
⅛ teaspoon pepper
1 tablespoon toasted almonds, chopped

1. Cut chicken into bite-size pieces. Brown chicken in hot oil in skillet, add stock, bring to a boil.
2. Stir in rice. Return to a boil.
3. Reduce heat to low; cover and simmer 5 minutes. Remove from heat.
4. Stir in parsley, lemon peel, and pepper; cover.
5. Let stand 5 minutes.
6. Sprinkle with almonds.

Here's a complete meal in one pot! Filling and heart healthy

Serves 4

Calories per serving 474
Cholesterol, mg 65.3
Calories from fat, % 15
Sodium, mg 81.7

Lime and chicken have been joined in culinary bliss for thousands of years from the Mediterranean to the Orient. Mashed potatoes flavored with lime zest are the perfect accoutrement.

LIME SAUCED

6 chicken breasts, boneless, skinless (4 ounces each)
Spice blend, freshly ground pepper to taste
1 tablespoon canola oil
Juice of 2 limes
1 tablespoon unsalted butter
1 tablespoon fresh chives, chopped
½ teaspoon fresh dill, chopped

1. Season chicken with spice blend and pepper.
2. In a skillet, heat oil on medium heat. Add chicken and sauté 4 minutes.
3. Turn chicken, cover skillet, reduce heat to low and cook until done (another 4–5 minutes).
4. Remove chicken. Discard oil from pan and wipe pan with paper towel.
5. Add lime juice and cook over low heat until bubbly. Add butter. Simmer until thickened.
6. Add chives and dill. Spoon over chicken.

Serves 6

Calories per serving 158
Cholesterol, mg 69.2
Calories from fat, % 30
Sodium, mg 74

MACEDONIAN

4 chicken breasts, skinless, boneless (4–6 ounces each)
⅓ cup fresh lemon juice
3 cloves garlic, finely chopped
1 teaspoon sweet paprika
½ teaspoon hot Hungarian paprika (red pepper flakes,
paprika, or chili powder may be substituted)
Pinch of ground allspice or cinnamon
1 cup plain, non-fat yogurt

1. Mix lemon juice, garlic, paprika, allspice (or cinnamon).
2. Coat chicken breasts with mixture. Cover and refrigerate overnight.
3. Heat and reduce yogurt until it measures ½ cup.
4. Bring chicken to room temperature.
5. Start grill or light broiler. Brush broiling or grilling rack with oil and set about 6" from heat source.
6. Place chicken on grill, coat with yogurt, and grill or broil, basting often and turning once or twice, until chicken is very tender, about half an hour.

Called "golden chicken" by the Macedonians because of the crisp, golden appearance. Serve with boiled potatoes, onions, and hot peppers mashed to a puree and seasoned with a touch of olive oil, vinegar, and garlic!

Serves 4
Calories per serving 175
Cholesterol, mg 71.5
Calories from fat, % 13
Sodium, mg 120

You'll find the original recipe at the famous all-night market in the center of Kuala Lumpur. Watch out, though...that one is definitely not heart healthy!
As with many dishes, serve simply with white rice.

MALAYSIAN WITH PEANUTS

1 pound chicken breasts, boneless, skinless,
2 teaspoons low-sodium soy sauce
1 tablespoon Chinese rice wine
4 green onions, cut into 1" pieces
1 teaspoon fresh ginger, peeled and minced
1 teaspoon nutmeg
½ cup orange juice
2 ½ teaspoons cornstarch
2 teaspoons canola oil
½ cup fresh snow peas
1 red pepper, cut into thin strips
1 ounce chopped roasted peanuts

1. Cut chicken into thin strips.
2. Mix soy, rice wine, green onions, nutmeg, and ginger. Add chicken and toss well.
3. Combine orange juice and cornstarch. Set aside.
4. Heat oil in large skillet or wok. Stir-fry chicken with marinade until chicken loses its color, about 2 minutes.
5. Add pea pods, red pepper, and peanuts.
6. Stir orange juice mixture and add to chicken.
7. Continue cooking until thickened.

Serves 4

Calories per serving 247
Cholesterol, mg 65.7
Calories from fat, % 28
Sodium, mg 162

MARBELLA

1½ pounds chicken breasts, skinless, cut into pieces
1–2 cloves garlic, peeled, finely pureed
⅛ cup dried oregano
¼ cup red wine vinegar
1 ounce olive oil
½ cup pitted prunes
11 ounces capers, drained
3 bay leaves
½ cup packed brown sugar
½ cup white wine
⅛ cup chopped parsley or cilantro

1. Preheat oven to 350°.
2. In a large bowl, combine chicken, garlic, oregano, vinegar, oil, prunes, capers, and bay leaves. Cover and allow to marinate, refrigerated, overnight.
3. Arrange chicken in a single layer in shallow baking pan and spoon marinade evenly. Sprinkle chicken pieces with brown sugar.
4. Pour white wine over top.
5. Bake 45 minutes, basting frequently with pan juices.
6. Remove chicken with slotted spoon.
7. Transfer chicken, prunes, olives, and capers to serving dish. Moisten with pan juices. Sprinkle generously with parsley or cilantro.

This one dates to Napoleon himself.
Serve it with the bones in…or Bonaparte.
It's great with oven roasted potatoes.

Serves 6
Calories per serving 288
Cholesterol, mg 65.7
Calories from fat, % 21
Sodium, mg 185

A lovely young woman I know who studies people's habits. Who's studying hers?

MARLA'S

4 chicken breasts, boneless, skinless (about 6 ounces each)
3 tablespoons annato oil*
4 cloves garlic
6 ounces orange juice
¼ cup lime juice
Spice blend, pepper to taste
2 banana leaves, cut in half**

1. Place the chicken breasts in a casserole dish.
2. Place the oil, garlic, orange juice, lime juice, spice blend and pepper in a blender and blend until smooth.
3. Pour the blended liquid over the chicken and marinate overnight.
4. The next day, steam the banana leaves until soft. Wrap each breast in a banana leaf. Brush the marinade on top of the breasts, then wrap in the banana leaves.
5. Fold the leaf package into a square shape and tie together with kitchen string.
6. Steam the packages for 1 hour or bake at 325° for 1 hour.

Serves 4

Calories per serving 201
Cholesterol, mg 68
Calories from fat, % 30
Sodium, mg 77

*To make annato oil, put 1 cup of annato seeds into 2 cups of vegetable oil. Let sit 15 minutes and strain.
**Can be found in most Latin American or Asian markets.

MEXICAN ALMOND

1½ pounds chicken breasts
1 large onion, quartered
6 to 8 lettuce leaves
½ cup fresh cilantro leaves
1 large clove garlic
2 teaspoons virgin olive oil
2 ounces ground almonds
12 corn tortillas, warmed
Guacamole (optional)*
2 cups low-fat sour cream (optional)*
1 cup cold water

1. Place chicken in single layer in large pot. Pour in water.
2. Bring to a boil, reduce heat, cover, and simmer 35–45 minutes or until tender. Cool in stock.
3. Remove chicken, retaining stock, discard skin and bones. Tear chicken into bite-size pieces.

Sauce:
1. Combine onion, lettuce, cilantro, garlic, and process until smooth.
2. Add about 1 cup of reserved stock, a few tablespoons at a time, until mixture has the consistency of whipping cream. Set aside.
3. Heat oil in a medium, heavy saucepan. Add almonds, lightly cook, and stir over medium heat just long enough to slightly toast almonds.
4. Add green sauce and cooled chicken and simmer 10–15 minutes.
5. Serve in warm tortillas, top with a dab of guacamole and low-fat sour cream, if desired.

*Nutrional information does not include guacamole or sour cream.

There are a lot of ingredients in this recipe, but it's well worth the effort. Serve with tortillas and salsa.

Serves 6
Calories per serving 271
Cholesterol, mg 65.3
Calories from fat, % 29
Sodium, mg 78.4

A one-pot meal from those wonderful folks who gave us Casablanca.
Serve the stew with couscous or flat bread.

MOROCCAN STEW WITH ONIONS AND GARBANZO BEANS

1½ pounds chicken breasts, skinless, boneless
3 tablespoons olive oil
3 large onions, chopped
3 tablespoons garlic chopped
2 teaspoons ground ginger
1 teaspoon turmeric
¼ teaspoon ground saffron
3 cups water
16-ounce can garbanzo beans, rinsed, drained
½ cup fresh Italian parsley, chopped
⅓ cup fresh cilantro, chopped

1. Heat oil in a large Dutch oven over medium-high heat.
2. Add onions, garlic, ginger, turmeric, and saffron; sauté until onions are translucent, about 5 minutes.
3. Add chicken and cook until brown on all sides, about 10 minutes.
4. Add 3 cups water and bring to boil.
5. Reduce heat, cover, and simmer until chicken is cooked through, about 40 minutes. Using tongs, transfer chicken to platter.
6. Add garbanzo beans, parsley, and cilantro to pot.
7. Boil until sauce thickens slightly, about 20 minutes.
8. Return chicken to pot.
9. Simmer until heated through, about 5 minutes.

Serves 6

Calories per serving 324
Cholesterol, mg 65.3
Calories from fat, % 28
Sodium, mg 79.4

MOROCCAN

1½ pounds chicken breasts, skinless, boneless
2 teaspoons olive oil
1 celery stalk, chopped
2 medium yellow onions chopped
1 cup low-salt tomato sauce
4 whole garlic cloves, peeled
½ orange, sliced with peel
1" cinnamon stick, broken into two
1 tablespoon dried oregano
½ cup raisins
½ cup pine nuts
1 teaspoon ground allspice

1. Preheat oven to 350°.
2. Brown chicken pieces in olive oil in Dutch oven. Do not overcrowd. Remove and keep warm.
3. Dispose of all but 2 tablespoons of fat, and sauté celery with onion until transparent.
4. Deglaze pan with tomato sauce. Add remaining ingredients and mix.
5. Return chicken to pot and toss well.
6. Cover and bake 30–45 minutes or until chicken is tender.
7. Remove cinnamon stick and garlic.

Play this one again, Sam. It's a Middle Eastern feast. Serve with rice pilaf.

Serves 8
Calories per serving 258
Cholesterol, mg 65.7
Calories from fat, % 29
Sodium, mg 88.4

A masterpiece! The sweetness of the roasted garlic will help make this unforgettable. Serve with mashed potatoes and a nice green vegetable.

"MUD" CHICKEN

2 pounds chicken breasts, skinless, boneless
3 heads of garlic (about 50 cloves)
1 tablespoon spice blend
2 ounces olive oil (or as needed)
1 cup all-purpose flour

1. Preheat oven to 325°.
2. Put peeled garlic cloves in a blender with olive oil and spice blend.
3. Blend until creamy consistency, add more oil if needed.
4. Place the oil and garlic mixture in a large bowl.
5. Add flour slowly, mixing until a very heavy, thick, smooth mudlike consistency is achieved.
6. Using a spatula, completely coat chicken pieces with garlic "mud," as evenly as possible (using it all).
7. Place in a roasting pan and put in preheated oven.
8. Roast chicken breast about 40–50 minutes or until coating is browned well.
9. Serve chicken with the crisp pieces of garlic coating.

A lower heat setting with a longer roast time is even better.

Serves 8

Calories per serving 321
Cholesterol, mg 65.7
Calories from fat, % 25
Sodium, mg 82.7

MUSTARD

Simple and delicious. Served with a spinach salad—it's a classic.

6 chicken breasts, boneless, skinless (4–6 ounces each)
1 teaspoon olive oil
1 teaspoon thyme
8 ounces water
½ cup onion, chopped
¼ cup Chinese-style mustard
2 teaspoons Worcestershire sauce
⅛ teaspoon Tabasco sauce
2 teaspoons unsalted butter

1. In a skillet, melt oil and unsalted butter.
2. Add chicken and sprinkle with thyme. Cook 10 minutes.
3. In a bowl, combine water, onion, mustard, Worcestershire sauce, and Tabasco sauce. Pour mixture over chicken.
4. Remove chicken, and transfer to a serving platter.
5. Boil remaining liquid on high heat until it reaches sauce consistency, 7–10 minutes. Pour sauce over chicken.

Serves 6

Calories per serving 168
Cholesterol, mg 68.8
Calories from fat, % 20
Sodium, mg 74.7

Ah, Naples. A jewel in Italy's crown. Serve with pasta and a salad. Gracie!

NEAPOLITAN

1½ pounds chicken breasts, skinless, boneless
2 tablespoons dried oregano, crushed,
1 tablespoon olive oil
2 large lemons
2 teaspoons garlic, finely minced
Freshly ground pepper to taste

1. Preheat oven to 500°.
2. Rinse and dry chicken. Arrange in shallow baking pan.
3. Mix oregano, oil, juice from 1 lemon, garlic, and pepper. Pour over chicken and marinate for several hours.
4. Bake 15 minutes, turn, and drizzle on remaining marinade. Continue cooking until chicken is done, 15–20 minutes.
5. Cut remaining lemon into wedges and serve with chicken.

Serves 4
Calories per serving 235
Cholesterol, mg 98.6
Calories from fat, % 23
Sodium, mg 112

NICARAGUAN CHICKEN AND CORN CASSEROLE

From Latin America comes this peasant offering. There's nothing ordinary about the flavor, though.

1 pound chicken breasts, skinless, boneless
1 pound chicken thighs, skinless, boneless
Nonstick spray
Spice blend, pepper to taste
1½ cups chicken stock
2 tablespoons cornstarch
1½ cups fresh corn kernels (or frozen)
4 sliced green ancho chilies (or more to taste), seeded and deveined

1. Preheat oven to 350°.
2. Rinse and pat dry chicken pieces. Rub with spice blend and pepper.
3. Spray pan with nonstick spray.
4. Brown slowly 10–15 minutes on all sides. Set aside and keep warm.
5. Mix the cornstarch, stock, corn, and chilies in a saucepan. Season with spice blend and pepper to taste. Cook over medium heat 10 minutes.
6. Place the chicken in a casserole, and pour corn and chili sauce over the top. Cover and bake in the oven 40–45 minutes. Serve right from the pot.

Serves 6

Calories per serving 296
Cholesterol, mg 115
Calories from fat, % 30
Sodium, mg 123

An incredibly easy, sticky-finger-lickin' kinda happiness for ya! Serve with mashed potatoes, a crispy salad, and a crusty bread for moppin' up the sauce!

ORANGE CINNAMON CROCK-POT

6 chicken breasts, skinnless, 6 ounces each
1 cup chicken broth
2 ounces unsalted butter
2 cups orange juice
1 cup raisins
Spice blend to taste
¼ teaspoon cinnamon (or to taste)
2 tablespoons flour

1. Heat butter in a large skillet, and brown chicken.
2. Remove chicken pieces to Crock-Pot as they brown.
3. Combine all other ingredients, except flour; mix well and pour over chicken.
4. Cover pot, set on low, and cook 4–6 hours or until chicken is tender. Remove 1 cup of sauce from the pot and combine with flour, mixing well. Return sauce-flour mixture to pot.
5. Turn pot to high, and cook an additional half hour.

Serves 6
Calories per serving 327
Cholesterol, mg 89
Calories from fat, % 26
Sodium, mg 81.9

ORANGE INFUSED

1½ pounds chicken breasts, skinless, boneless
1 lemon
2 oranges
Spice blend to taste
2 cloves garlic, minced
2 teaspoons paprika
1 teaspoon chili powder (or to taste)
1 teaspoon ground coriander
1 cup water
2 onions

1. Preheat oven to 350°.
2. Cut the lemon in half and rub ½ over chicken. Squeeze juice of the other half and 1 orange into bowl.
3. Put the chicken in a roasting pan. Mix spice blend, garlic, and spices together and sprinkle over chicken.
4. Pour the juice mix into pan around chicken. Add water. Cut onions in half and add to pan.
5. Cook chicken 15 minutes, baste with pan juices, and lower heat to 325°.
6. Roast 30 minutes, basting after 10 minutes.
7. Transfer to serving platter. Cut the whole orange and the halved onions into pieces and serve with the chicken.

Another old recipe I've borrowed from my grandmother. She had very discriminating taste…she married my grandfather!
Serve this over noodles.

Serves 6

Calories per serving 162
Cholesterol, mg 65.7
Calories from fat, % 9
Sodium, mg 74.8

One of the world's most exotic fruits, yet so available. Serve with garlic mashed potatoes and an orange-fennel salad.

PAPAYA WITH HONEY-NUTMEG GLAZE

6 chicken breasts, boneless (4–6 ounces each)
¾ cup honey
¼ cup freshly squeezed lime juice
3 teaspoons unsalted butter
¾ teaspoon freshly ground nutmeg
1 papaya, peeled and seeded
1 tablespoon canola oil
Raspberries (optional)

To make glaze:
1. Combine honey, lime juice, 2 teaspoons of butter, and nutmeg in saucepan. Cook over medium heat until thickened, stirring occasionally to blend. Dice three-quarters of papaya and slice the remaining into thin wedges.

1. Preheat oven to 350°.
2. Heat remaining butter and oil in skillet. Sauté chicken breasts until golden brown.
3. Place chicken in large baking dish. Bake 10 minutes. Cover with glaze and diced papaya. Continue baking until chicken is tender, another 10 minutes or so. Serve hot. garnished with sliced papaya and raspberries.

Serves 6

Calories per serving 275
Cholesterol, mg 73.2
Calories from fat, % 19
Sodium, mg 79.1

PARISIAN BISTRO

2 pounds chicken breasts, boneless, skinless
4 tablespoons arrowroot
Spice blend to taste
¼ teaspoon freshly ground pepper
2 cups water
1 cup dry red wine
½ teaspoon sage
2 bay leaves
pinch of thyme
1 cup unsalted tomato-vegetable juice

1. Preheat oven to 450°.
2. Combine arrowroot, spice blend, and pepper in a large paper grocery bag.
3. Add all the chicken pieces, close the bag tightly, and shake until all the chicken breasts have been lightly coated.
4. Place the chicken breast, skin side down, on a nonstick cookie sheet. Bake in the oven 15 minutes, turning once.
5. Reduce the oven temperature to 350°. Discard any melted fat.
6. Put the browned chicken pieces in an ovenproof casserole dish and add the remaining ingredients, except the tomato juice.
7. Cover and bake 20 minutes.
8. Uncover, add the tomato juice, and continue the baking until the liquid evaporates into a thick sauce.

Ah, "l'amour du poulet" or "Charles de Gaulle" or whatever one should say when toasting the French! There are some givens in this world. One of them is that you'll find this dish (though not as healthily prepared) in every bistro in Paris. Serve with crusty French bread and a tomato salad.

Serves 6
Calories per serving 308
Cholesterol, mg 150
Calories from fat, % 14
Sodium, mg 171

The Pawnee were a settled, agricultural people, occupying large, relatively permanent villages in what are now Nebraska and Oklahoma. Here's a complete meal to please your own tribe.

PAWNEE

4-pound chicken
Spice blend and freshly ground pepper to taste
2 cups celery, diced
2 cups onion, diced
3–4 tablespoons fresh sage chopped (or 3–4 teaspoons dried)
6 tablespoons honey
4 medium-size sweet potatoes
2 tablespoons freshly chopped chives
1 tablespoon hulled sunflower seeds lightly toasted

1. Preheat oven to 350°.
2. Rinse chicken and pat dry, and place in roasting pan.
3. Season cavity with spice blend and freshly ground pepper to taste.
4. Mix celery, onion, and sage together and stuff cavity with mixture.
5. Truss chicken securely.
6. Brush chicken with honey.
7. Roast 20 minutes per pound or until the juices run clear from the thickest part of the thigh when pierced with a knife.
8. Baste occasionally with pan juices.
9. Scrub potatoes and prick once or twice with a fork.
10. Roast potatoes in oven with chicken 45–60 minutes or until fork tender.
11. Slit potatoes when done and carefully push ends toward the middle, opening them. Drizzle with remaining honey and sprinkle with chives and sunflower seeds.

Serves 8

Calories per serving 398
Cholesterol, mg 127
Calories from fat, % 26
Sodium, mg 155

PEANUT BUTTER

This one's more Oriental than you'd think. You know what that means...rice!

2½ pounds chicken breasts, skinless, cut into pieces
½ cup onion, chopped
3 ounces unsalted low-fat peanut butter
½ tablespoon low-sodium soy sauce
1 tablespoon brown sugar
2 tablespoons water
½ teaspoon garlic powder
1 tablespoon fresh lemon juice
½ teaspoon cinnamon
Vegetable cooking spray

1. Combine all ingredients, except chicken and onion, in a blender. Blend until smooth.
2. Place mixture in a saucepan and warm over low heat 5 minutes.
3. Place chicken in an 8" x 8" baking dish, sprayed with vegetable spray. Sprinkle onion on top and spread peanut butter mixture on top of everything. Marinate overnight.
4. Put baking dish in preheated 350° oven 45 minutes or until done.

Serves 8
Calories per serving 231
Cholesterol, mg 81.7
Calories from fat, % 28
Sodium, mg 126

How Latin American can you get? Serve with Latin-American couscous made with cornmeal and fresh vegetables.

PERUVIAN

3 pounds chicken breasts, skinless, cut into pieces
3 tablespoons unsalted butter
1 small onion, chopped
4 cloves
½ teaspoon cumin
4 ounces water
1¼ cups dry white wine
½ cup golden raisins
½ cup sliced almonds

1. In a heavy skillet heat butter and sauté chicken pieces over medium heat 4 minutes per side.
2. Add onions, cloves, cumin, and water. Cover and simmer on low heat 15 minutes.
3. Add wine, raisins, and almonds.
4. Increase heat to medium.
5. Cook partly covered 20 to 25 minutes.

Serves 6

Calories per serving 285
Cholesterol, mg 76
Calories from fat, % 27
Sodium, mg 80

PIRATE'S

This recipe was discovered in I Was Bluebeard's Colorist *(a little-known book found in a sunken pirate's ship). Serve with a fresh fruit salad .*

5 pounds chicken breasts, skinless
¾ teaspoon spice blend
½ cup brown sugar
2 tablespoons dark rum
1 tablespoon fresh lime juice
1 teaspoon fresh ginger, grated
½ teaspoon ground cloves
¼ teaspoon cinnamon
¼ teaspoon garlic powder
2 drops hot pepper sauce (or to taste)
Lemon, sliced
Lime, sliced
Parsley

1. Preheat oven to 400°.
2. Sprinkle spice blend over chicken. Set aside.
3. In a small bowl, make the "pirate's" paste by mixing together sugar, 2 tablespoons of the rum, lime juice, ginger, cloves, cinnamon, garlic powder, and hot pepper sauce.
4. Rub the "pirate" paste evenly over the chicken.
5. Place the chicken in a large shallow baking pan.
6. Bake in oven 30–45 minutes or until the chicken is fork tender.
7. Arrange chicken on a serving platter. Garnish with lime, lemon, and parsley.

Serves 10

Calories per serving 300
Cholesterol, mg 131
Calories from fat, % 9
Sodium, mg 152

Portugal doesn't seem to get nearly the culinary credit it deserves. This simple recipe goes well with saffroned rice and crusty bread. While you're at it, celebrate this beautiful land with a glass of lusty port.

PORTUGUESE

3 pounds chicken breasts, skinless
½ cup white wine
Spice blend to taste
3 garlic cloves chopped
1 tablespoon unsalted butter
2 tablespoons olive oil
2 bay leaves
Tabasco sauce to taste
1 cup chicken stock

1. Cut chicken into 6–8 pieces.
2. Marinate in wine, spice blend and garlic for two hours.
3. In a skillet, heat butter and olive oil. Add bay leaf and Tabasco. Add chicken.
4. Reduce heat, simmer 5 minutes. Add stock.
5. Cover and simmer 1 hour.

Serves 4
Calories per serving 323
Cholesterol, mg 131
Calories from fat, % 26
Sodium, mg 147

POULET AU SHALLOT

3 pounds chicken breasts, skinless cut into 6–8 pieces
3 tablespoons unsalted butter
6 shallots (3 minced, 3 left whole)
4 ounces dry white wine
Spice blend and freshly ground pepper to taste

1. Melt the butter in a large skillet and sauté the pieces of chicken until nicely browned. Remove them from the pan and sauté the chopped and the whole shallots just until they turn brown.
2. Season chicken with spice blend and freshly ground pepper.
3. Return the chicken to the pan.
4. Reduce heat and cook 45 minutes, turning the chicken occasionally.
5. As soon as the juices from the chicken start to dry, add the wine and cook a few minutes more, until the wine is reduced by about one-third.
6. Discard the whole shallots before serving.

Lots of shallots, lots of taste. Ah, those sneaky French! Serve this with mashed potatoes and a tomato salad.

Serves 6

Calories per serving 325
Cholesterol, mg 146
Calories from fat, % 24
Sodium, mg 150

What every busy French household serves. Throw a crusty French baguette in a basket and voilà!

POULET POUR LA FAMILLE

3 pounds chicken breasts, skinless, cut into pieces
8 roma tomatoes
3 tablespoons olive oil
1 onion, sliced
½ cup celery, sliced
½ cup chardonnay (or dry white wine)
1 teaspoon fresh oregano, chopped
2 tablespoons balsamic vinegar
1 cup mushrooms, sliced

1. Heat oil in a large saucepan and brown chicken lightly on both sides.
2. Add onion and celery and cook about two minutes.
3. Add the wine, oregano, and tomatoes; season with spice blend and pepper, and simmer, covered, about 30 minutes, turning chicken once.
4. Add balsamic vinegar and mushrooms, and cook another 5 minutes.

Serves 6

Calories per serving 360
Cholesterol, mg 131
Calories from fat, % 26
Sodium, mg 168

PRUNE STUFFED

3 pounds chicken breasts, skinless, boneless
1½ pounds prunes, pitted
Spice blend to taste
1 teaspoon sweet paprika
1 teaspoon black pepper
½ teaspoon oregano

1. Preheat oven to 350°.
2. Place prunes in a bowl and pour boiling water to cover. Let stand 1 hour. With a slotted spoon, remove the prunes. Set aside, reserving the liquid.
3. Place chicken breasts between sheets of waxed paper and flatten to ½" thickness. Sprinkle with a little spice blend, pepper and paprika.
4. Loosely stuff breasts with about half the prunes, fold in half, and secure with kitchen string.
5. Place stuffed chicken in an ovenproof casserole and roast 30 minutes, basting frequently with the prune liquid.
6. Add the remaining prunes to the casserole and continue roasting until the chicken is done (about 20 minutes longer). Serve hot.

No laughing. This is a very old recipe my grandmother gave me. She cut it out of a magazine, which is swell because she couldn't cook very well! Try it with potato pancakes and a salad.

Serves 4
Calories per serving 268
Cholesterol, mg 123
Calories from fat, % 8
Sodium, mg 133

PULLUM FRONTONIANUM
(ANCIENT ROME)

This recipe is so authentic that I've used the original Latin name. Serve this at your next toga party with a side order of lion!

2 pounds chicken breasts, skinless, boneless
3 ounces peanut oil
7 ounces red wine
2 teaspoons spice blend (original recipe used salt)
1 leek
Fresh bunches of dill and coriander,
Freshly ground black pepper to taste
A little bit of defritum (If available—but it's not—use 2 ounces of grape juice reduced by two-thirds.)

1. Preheat oven to 425°.
2. Mix oil and spice blend. Add to skillet.
3. When oil is heated, "paint" chicken breasts.
4. Place chicken breasts in casserole dish.
5. Add the dill, leek, and fresh coriander.
6. Roast chicken about 30 minutes or until internal temperature reaches 165°.
7. When the chicken is done, moisten a plate with defritum, put chicken on it, sprinkle with lots of freshly ground black pepper, and serve.

Serves 6–8

Calories per serving 230
Cholesterol, mg 75.1
Calories from fat, % 29
Sodium, mg 89.4

QUEBEC ROAST

1½ pounds chicken breasts, skinless
1 tablespoon oil
1 tablespoon unsalted butter
50 peeled garlic cloves
2 onions, peeled, quartered
3 tablespoons fresh rosemary, finely chopped
or tarragon or marjoram, or all three if you're brave
2 cups chicken stock
1 cup balsamic vinegar
Spice blend, freshly ground pepper to taste

1. Preheat oven to 450°.
2. Heat oil and butter in large skillet. Add garlic and onions. Brown slightly, remove with slotted spoon, draining excess fat. Portion one-half of the onions and garlic mixture atop each breast and add 2 tablespoons of herb. Roll breasts and secure with kitchen string or toothpicks.
3. Brush outside with remaining oil.
4. Place chicken in ovenproof roasting pan.
5. Add ½-cup stock and bake 1 hour.
6. Add 1 cup stock.
7. Cook another half hour, basting occasionally until thermometer reads 165–170°.
8. Remove chicken and set aside.
9. Pour rest of stock in pan. Add vinegar, remaining onion and garlic mixture from chicken, and herbs. Boil and reduce by half. Continue cooking until sauce thickens, skim off any fat and reseason with spice blend and pepper.

Fifty cloves of garlic? Maybe that's why the Canadians invented hockey…so they would have somebody to play with! Serve with a maple leaf salad—all right then, a green salad.

Serves 6
Calories per serving 256
Cholesterol, mg 73.2
Calories from fat, % 21
Sodium, mg 91

*Quinces are one of our least appreciated foods. Crunchy like apples...
but just different enough to surprise you. Serve with roasted potatoes and salad*

QUINCED

1½ *pounds chicken breasts, skinless, boneless, cut into pieces*
2 *quinces*
1 *tablespoon lemon juice*
¼ *cup all-purpose flour*
Spice blend and freshly ground black pepper to taste
2 *tablespoons olive oil*
1 *large onion, chopped*
2 *cloves garlic, chopped*
14*-ounce can Italian plum tomatoes*
1*" cinnamon stick*
Spice blend to taste
2 *tablespoons fresh mint, chopped*

1. Peel and core the quinces, cut into quarters, and then cut into thick slices.
2. Cover with cold water and lemon juice to prevent them turning brown.
3. Lightly dredge the chicken pieces with flour seasoned with spice blend and pepper.
4. Heat half the oil and brown the chicken on all sides.
5. Drain the quince slices and dry with a paper towel.
6. Remove the chicken pieces and lightly brown the quince slices, lift out with a slotted spoon and put to one side.
7. Add the rest of the olive oil, and gently cook the onion and garlic until soft but not brown.
8. Return the chicken pieces to the pan and stir in the tomatoes, squashing them against the side of the pan with a wooden spoon.
9. Add the cinnamon stick, a little water, and additional spice blend to taste.
10. Cover and simmer gently 20 minutes, then return the quince slices to the pan. Cook another 15 to 20 minutes, then stir in the chopped mint and cook another 5 minutes. Before serving remove the cinnamon stick.

Serves 4

Calories per serving 381
Cholesterol, mg 98.6
Calories from fat, % 23
Sodium, mg 136

RED WINE
(TUSCANY)

2 pounds chicken breasts, skinless
2 cups red wine
2 medium onions, chopped
2 cloves minced garlic
6-ounce can unsalted tomato-vegetable juice
1 teaspoon Dijon mustard
½ teaspoon dried thyme
¼ teaspoon ground allspice
½ pound fresh mushrooms

1. Combine all ingredients except mushrooms in a heavy Dutch oven. Cover and simmer 30 minutes.
2. Add mushrooms.
3. Simmer uncovered until liquid had reduced to a thick sauce, about 20–25 minutes.
4. Spoon over noodles.

The foods of Tuscany reflect Italy's best home cooking. It's robust, it's simple, and it's always in season. Serve over noodles…home-made, maybe? Bella!

Serves 6

Calories per serving 250
Cholesterol, mg 87.6
Calories from fat, % 8
Sodium, mg 126

Here's a grand example of how flavorful Indian food can be...and not rely on a curry flavor. Serve with basmati rice, warmed pita bread, and chutneys.

RESHMI KABOBS
(BOMBAY)

2 pounds chicken breasts, ground
4 medium-size onions
2" ginger
8 cloves garlic
1 bunch cilantro leaves
1 teaspoon cumin seeds
1 teaspoon white pepper or to taste
1 teaspoon garam masala (available in Indian grocery stores)
2 eggs
Spice blend to taste
Lemon and spring onions for garnishing

1. Mix all ingredients together except eggs and spice blend.
2. Mix in the eggs and spice blend.
3. Shape into sausages, fold around skewers, and cook over charcoal fire till done.
4. Garnish with onions and lemon.

Cumin

Serves 4

Calories per serving 241
Cholesterol, mg 159
Calories from fat, % 15
Sodium, mg 124

RENAISSANCE ORANGE

5-pound chicken, cut into 10–12 pieces
⅓ cup arrowroot
1 tablespoon spice blend
2 teaspoons unsalted butter
¾ cup chicken stock
½ cup dry white wine
1½ cups orange juice
2 ½ teaspoons dried orange peel
⅛ teaspoon ground rosemary
⅛ teaspoon cinnamon
⅛ teaspoon ground ginger
1 teaspoon sugar
1 cup pitted prunes
½ cup currants
Generous pinch of mace
Orange slices

1. Sprinkle chicken lightly with spice blend and dredge in arrowroot.
2. In a heavy skillet, melt butter. Brown chicken, set aside.
3. In a large enameled pot, combine remaining ingredients (except orange slices). Bring to boil, reduce flame, and simmer.
4. Add browned chicken pieces, cover, and simmer about 1 hour or until chicken is tender.
5. Taste test the seasoning.
6. Arrange pieces of chicken on bed of rice or noodles and spoon orange sauce on top. Garnish with orange slices.

The Renaissance ended the Dark Ages. What a way to come to life! This recipe is spectacular. If you can't find currants, use raisins, but currants are better. Serve on a bed of noodles with orange sauce spooned over, then go out and paint a ceiling!

Serves 6–8

Calories per serving 407
Cholesterol, mg 170
Calories from fat, % 26
Sodium, mg 178

From northern Italy, this heart-healthy gem is easy to prepare and easier to enjoy. Mange!

RICOTTA AND NUTMEG STUFFED

3–4 pounds chicken breasts, boneless, skinless
1 tablespoon olive oil
¼ teaspoon tarragon
¼ teaspoon paprika
¼ teaspoon oregano
Spice blend, pepper to taste
4 ounces low-fat ricotta cheese
½ pound spinach, boiled and chopped
Egg substitute (equivalent to 1 egg)
Nutmeg to taste

1. Preheat oven to 375°.
2. Carefully slice breasts to form pocket. Rub oil, tarragon, paprika and oregano on breast pieces.
3. Mix ricotta, spinach, egg, and nutmeg.
4. Stuff mixture in pocket of chicken.
5. Place breasts inovenproof baking dish. Roast 10 minutes.
6. Lower oven temperature to 350°. Roast an additional 20 minutes.

Serves 6

Calories 232
Cholesterol, mg 95.2
Calories from fat, % 27
Sodium, mg 136

ROMAN

1½ pounds chicken breast, skinless, boneless, cut into pieces
1 tablespoon olive oil
3 cloves garlic, chopped
1 tablespoon red bell pepper chopped
½ cup chopped rosemary
¼ cup fresh lemon juice
½ cup chicken stock
4 ounces water
10 capers (OK, 11 if you're brave!)
1 tablespoon oregano
1 ounce anchovies, rinsed and drained
1 cup red wine vinegar

1. Brown chicken pieces in oil.
2. Add 2 cloves garlic, red pepper, rosemary, and lemon juice to pan. Bring to a boil over high heat. Add chicken stock and capers, cover pan. Lower heat and simmer 45 minutes.
3. Press remaining garlic, oregano, and drained anchovies until they form a paste. Add vinegar and process mixture until smooth. Allow pureed mixture to sit 30 minutes.
4. Remove chicken to a dish.

For the sauce:
Add pureed mixture to pan and boil until reduced by half. Spoon over chicken just before serving.

You'll have your family and guests roamin' around looking for seconds with this one. Keep it simple, with a lettuce, tomato, and fresh basil salad.

Serves 6
Calories per serving 155
Cholesterol, mg 65.7
Calories from fat, % 22
Sodium, mg 174

When the Ottoman Turks
invaded the Roman Empire
in the 14th century,
they turned away from the
Moslem religion and took
Romanian food instead!
The strong Middle Eastern
influence is quite noticeable.
Serve this beaut with corn
bread and a salad.

ROMANIAN

2½ pounds chicken breasts, skinless
2 medium onions, peeled, sliced thin
2 cloves garlic, crushed
1½ tablespoons olive oil
2 cups dry white wine
4 ounces fresh parsley, chopped
2 ounces low-fat sour cream at room temperature

1. Sauté the onions and garlic in a large skillet in hot oil.
   Don't let garlic brown!
2. Add the chicken pieces and brown on all sides.
3. Add the wine. Mix well. Cover and cook one hour.
4. Add the parsley and sour cream. Cook another 5 minutes
   or until the chicken is tender.

Parsley

Serves 8

Calories per serving 245
Cholesterol, mg 82.2
Calories from fat, % 21
Sodium, mg 108

ROSE PETAL

1 pound chicken breasts, boneless, skinless
Petals from 2 roses, crushed just enough
to release aroma and natural oils
½ tablespoon unsalted butter
1 clove garlic, crushed
½ ounce almonds, slivered
1 tablespoon honey

1. Sauté breasts in half the butter on medium heat until golden (4–5 minutes on each side). Set aside.
2. Sauté garlic in remaining butter 1 minute. Add almonds and cook 2 more minutes. Remove from heat.
3. Gently stir in rose petals and honey.
4. Spoon sauce over chicken and serve with a kiss.

A delicious blend of East and West, to be served with lots of love. The perfect Valentine's Day dinner with candlelight.

Serves 2
Calories per serving 239
Cholesterol, mg 73.5
Calories from fat, % 30
Sodium, mg 75.9

SANTA FE SALSA

4 chicken breasts, skinless, boneless (4–6 ounces each)
Salsa
2 green onions, minced
1 large tomato, diced
1 clove garlic, minced
Minced jalapeño pepper to taste
⅓ cup fresh, canned, or frozen corn
2 tablespoons olive or canola oil, divided
2 tablespoons lemon juice, divided
¼ teaspoon cumin
2 tablespoons fresh cilantro, chopped

1. Combine salsa ingredients using half each of the oil and lemon juice and cilantro. Cover and chill for several hours, remove 1 hour before serving. Pound chicken flat to ¼" thickness.
2. Combine remaining oil, lemon juice, and cilantro. Pour over chicken. Chill 2 hours. Barbecue 5–7 minutes per side. Serve warm with tortillas and salsa

Serves 4

Calories per serving 474
Cholesterol, mg 173
Calories from fat, % 23
Sodium, mg 188

SHAKER CIDER BREASTS

3 pounds chicken breasts, skinless
2 teaspoons unsalted butter
¼ cup onions, finely chopped
¼ cup carrots, finely chopped
4 cups mushrooms, finely chopped
1 cup apples, finely chopped
1 tablespoon flour
Bouquet garni (1 bay leaf; ½ teaspoon each parsley,
thyme, tarragon, tied together)
1½ cups apple juice
1 cup buttermilk
Parsley for garnish (optional)

1. Brown chicken in butter in a large, heavy pot.
2. Add vegetables, apples, flour, and bouquet garni. Pour in juice.
3. Cover and cook 20–30 minutes, or until chicken is cooked through.
4. Remove chicken and add buttermilk to the liquid in the pot; simmer until sauce is reduced and thickened.
5. Return chicken to sauce to heat.
6. Serve chicken pieces individually, or arrange on a platter and pour sauce over all.
7. Garnish with parsley, if desired.

Along with creating simply designed furniture, the Shakers created simply designed recipes. This one needs only a loaf of crusty bread.

Serves 8
Calories per serving 368
Cholesterol, mg 149
Calories from fat, % 23
Sodium, mg 170

Have you ever been smothered by a roast chicken? I'd certainly like to hear about it. In the meantime, this complete meal is as enjoyable as the fibs you'll make up about how much time you spent preparing it.

SMOTHERED ROAST CHICKEN AND POTATOES

2 pounds chicken breasts, skinless, boneless
3 tablespoons olive oil
8 red potatoes, halved
3 medium red onions, quartered
1 tablespoon fresh or 2 teaspoons dried rosemary
2 large cloves finely chopped garlic
Nonstick spray

1. Preheat oven to 325°.
2. Spray 9" x 13" baking dish with no-fat nonstick spray.
3. Sprinkle potatoes and onions with spice blend and pepper. Place potatoes in the center of an oiled baking dish. Sprinkle rosemary and garlic over potatoes.
4. Spread chicken breasts over potatoes. Arrange onions around edges. Drizzle and rub olive oil over chicken.
5. Roast 35–40 minutes. Pour off all liquids and garnish with fresh rosemary sprigs. Serve hot or cold.

Serves 6
Calories per serving 274
Cholesterol, mg 87.6
Calories from fat, % 30
Sodium, mg 101

SPANISH SAFFRONED

1½ pounds chicken breasts, boneless, skinless
¼ cup seasoned flour
1 teaspoon spice blend
1 teaspoon freshly ground black pepper
1 tablespoon olive oil
1 cup onions, diced
1 cup water
¼ cup sherry
1 hard-cooked egg yoke
2 tablespoons almonds, chopped
2 cloves garlic
2 tablespoons parsley, chopped
Generous dash of crushed saffron or turmeric

1. Mix flour, spice blend, freshly ground black pepper.
2. Dust chicken with flour and brown in hot oil.
3. Add onions, water, sherry, and parsley. Cover and cook, stirring occasionally, over low heat 45 minutes or until chicken is done.
4. Combine egg yolk, almonds, garlic, and saffron. Stir into the sauce to thicken and heat, stirring occasionally.

The Arabs controlled Spain for 600 years. Go figure...culinary-wise! Serve this delicate dish with a great big side of rice and a nice Spanish wine.

Serves 4
Calories per serving 314
Cholesterol, mg 151
Calories from fat, % 26
Sodium, mg 122

Even if don't have a tandoor oven, this one's absolutely spectacular with the ever-complementary basmati rice and chutney selection.

SPICY TANDOORI

1 pound chicken breasts, skinless, boneless
1 pound chicken thighs, skinless, boneless
½ cup plain, low-fat yogurt
Juice and grated peel of 1 lemon
2 teaspoons each paprika, ground cumin, and coriander
1 teaspoon freshly ground pepper
½ teaspoon pumpkin pie spice
½ teaspoon allspice
Pinch cayenne pepper (or more to taste)

1. With sharp knife, make several cuts into meat.
2. Combine remaining ingredients, and pour over chicken in glass or plastic bowl and refrigerate all day, or overnight, turning occasionally.
3. Remove chicken from marinade and discard marinade.
4. Grill chicken about 6" from charcoal, turning each piece frequently, 30–40 minutes, until golden brown.

Serves 6
Calories per serving 138
Cholesterol, mg 66.5
Calories from fat, % 12
Sodium, mg 86.5

SRI LANKAN

2 pounds chicken breasts, boneless, skinless, cut into pieces
Spice blend
1 tablespoon lemon juice
1 seeded, roughly chopped green chili
1 ounce fresh, peeled gingerroot
3 small garlic cloves, peeled
1 pint plain low-fat yogurt
2 teaspoons paprika
1 teaspoon chili powder
Orange food coloring
2 tablespoons unsalted butter, melted
1 pint low-fat sour cream

1. Preheat oven 350°.
2. With a sharp knife, make regular slits through the flesh of chicken pieces.
3. Rub with spice blend, then sprinkle with lemon juice.
4. Process the green chili, ginger, and garlic to a fine paste. Mix paste with yogurt, paprika, chili powder, and a few drops of orange food coloring.
5. Place the chicken portions and spice mixture in large bowl.
6. Cover and marinate 4–5 hours.
7. Remove chicken portions, place in greased baking tray, and cook in oven 45–50 minutes.
8. Brush the portions occasionally with a little melted butter. Melt the unsalted butter in a saucepan, add remaining marinade and sour cream.
9. Gently heat, without boiling 5–6 minutes.
10. Pour sauce over baked chicken and serve.

A grand, colorful dish with the right amount of spice. Serve with nan bread (available at Indian stores) or pita and rice.

Serves 8
Calories per serving 190
Cholesterol, mg 74.9
Calories from fat, % 23
Sodium, mg 105

STOVIES
(SCOTLAND)

2 pounds chicken breasts, skinless, boneless
4 onions sliced into half-rounds
4 large potatoes sliced into thin rounds
Spice blend and freshly ground pepper to taste
2 ounces unsalted butter
1 cup chicken stock

1. Arrange chicken pieces, potato, and onion slices in layers in a heavy iron pan or Dutch oven.
2. Dot each layer with butter and sprinkle with spice blend and freshly ground pepper.
3. Moisten with enough chicken stock to prevent chicken, potatoes, and onions from burning.
4. Cover tightly and simmer over low heat one hour or until the chicken and potatoes are tender.

Serves 4

Calories per serving 471
Cholesterol, mg 96.8
Calories from fat, % 25
Sodium, mg 93.4

ST. THOMAS BANANA AND RUM

3–4-pound roasting chicken
Spice blend and freshly ground black pepper to taste

Stuffing:
  1 tablespoon unsalted butter
  2 cloves garlic
  1 cup bread crumbs
  ¼ cup lime juice
  1 tablespoon dark rum
  1 tablespoon grated lime zest
  1 teaspoon brown sugar
  ¼ teaspoon each nutmeg and cayenne pepper
  4 ripe bananas, peeled and chopped

1. Preheat oven to 350°.
2. Wash chicken, sprinkle inside and out with spice blend and pepper.
3. Melt butter on medium heat. Add garlic, cook 1 minute.
4. Add bread crumbs, cook until crisp and brown. Remove from pan.
5. Stir in lime juice, zest, rum, brown sugar, nutmeg, and cayenne pepper. Mix well. Add bananas and toss to combine.
6. Stuff chicken and truss. Place chicken in roasting pan.
7. Brush the remaining unsalted butter on chicken, roast 2 hours, until the thermometer reads 185°.

Can you hear the lush palm trees in the background? Can you smell the ocean? OK, can you smell the palm trees and hear the ocean ? Enjoy this tropical treat served with a fresh fruit salad.

Serves 6
Calories per serving 350
Cholesterol, mg 107
Calories from fat, % 30
Sodium, mg 137

Here's a variation of Chinese cooking from the island of Taiwan. Serve with rice and perhaps a green leafy Chinese vegetable.

TAIWAN LEMON SAUCE

1 pound chicken breasts, boneless, skinless
2 tablespoons canola oil
2 cloves garlic, chopped
1 tablespoon low-sodium soy sauce
1 large onion, sliced
1 lemon, cut into 3 wedges
½ cup chicken stock
1 tablespoon cornstarch
3 tablespoons water
1 minced green onion (scallion)

1. Cut chicken into thin strips, about 3" long.
2. Heat oil in skillet over medium heat. Add chicken, small amounts at a time. Add garlic and sauté with meat 2 minutes.
3. Mix in soy sauce. Add onion and cook 1 minute.
4. Squeeze lemon over mixture, and add wedges to pan. Add stock and mix well.
5. Remove and discard lemon wedges.
6. Combine water with cornstarch. Stir into skillet and cook, stirring, until sauce thickens. Garnish with green onions.

Serves 6
Calories per serving 216
Cholesterol, mg 43.6
Calories from fat, % 24
Sodium, mg 107

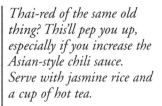

THAI BARBECUED

1½ pounds chicken breasts, boneless, skinless, 4–6 ounces

Marinade:
2 teaspoons Thai curry powder (or to taste)(available at Asian grocery stores)
1 teaspoon turmeric
¼ teaspoon black pepper
3 ounces evaporated milk
2 ounces freshly shredded coconut
3 tablespoons cilantro, minced (including stems)
3 tablespoons garlic, minced
3 tablespoons onion, minced
1 tablespoon sugar

For the apricot sauce:
½ cup low-calorie apricot preserves or jam
¼ cup low-calorie apricot nectar
1 teaspoon Thai or Chinese-style chili sauce

1. Preheat oven to 350F.
2. Combine all ingredients, except those for apricot sauce.
3. Rub marinade over chicken, and refrigerate at least 4 hours or, for best results, overnight, covered.
4. Roast chicken 30 minutes.
5. Remove from oven. Turn oven to broil and broil chicken 3–5 minutes on each side until dark golden brown.
6. Serve with apricot sauce.

Thai-red of the same old thing? This'll pep you up, especially if you increase the Asian-style chili sauce. Serve with jasmine rice and a cup of hot tea.

Serves 4
Calories per serving 244
Cholesterol, mg 69.9
Calories from fat, % 22
Sodium, mg 99.7

This one's named for the woman who makes me beautiful (despite what she has to work with!). Her special beauty is inside. Serve over pasta with a green salad and warm, crunchy bread.

TINA'S

1 pound chicken breasts, boneless, skinless,
(4–6 ounces each)
Spice blend and freshly ground pepper to taste
1 tablespoon olive oil
16 garlic cloves, thinly sliced, blanched
1 tablespoon unsalted butter
1 teaspoon minced fresh sage
Juice of 1½ lemons
1 teaspoon Italian parsley, minced

1. Preheat the oven to 450°.
2. Season chicken breasts with spice blend and pepper.
3. Heat a large ovenproof sauté pan over moderately high heat until hot. Add oil and heat until hot. Add chicken and sear. Turn chicken and place pan in oven.
4. Bake 15 to 20 minutes or until cooked through.
5. Drop garlic cloves in boiling water for 10 seconds, remove with slotted spoon, and drop into ice water.
6. In a small saucepan combine garlic, butter, and sage. Heat, whisking vigorously. Add lemon juice and parsley.
7. Drizzle over chicken.

Serves 4

Calories per serving 182
Cholesterol, mg 70.5
Calories from fat, % 28
Sodium, mg 75.5

TUNISIAN SWEET-SPICED BREASTS

4 chicken breasts, skinless (4–6 ounces each)
3 large cloves garlic, minced
2 green onions, minced
1 teaspoon ground cinnamon
1 teaspoon ground allspice
1 teaspoon coarsely cracked pepper
1 tablespoon canola oil
2 large onions, thinly sliced
½ cup golden raisins
2 tablespoons cider vinegar
1 tablespoon parsley, minced

1. Preheat oven to 400°.
2. Combine garlic, green onions, cinnamon, allspice, pepper, and oil in small bowl, blend into a paste and rub over breasts.
3. Arrange onion slices, separated into rings, in center of four heavy-duty aluminum foil sheets. Add raisins and sprinkle vinegar on top.
4. Place breasts on top of onions and raisins.
5. Tent foil so that a small amount of air remains between the foil and chicken.
6. Place foil packages on baking sheet.
7. Bake 45 minutes.
8. Arrange on plates and spoon onion, raisins, and juices over each breast.

This dish is surprisingly mild with none of the hot chilies other African recipes call for. As with Algerian and Moroccan food, Tunisian is multilayered in flavors and lends itself perfectly to couscous.

Serves 4
Calories per serving 270
Cholesterol, mg 68
Caloriesfrom fat 17
Sodium, mg 82.3

Turkish cuisine has its roots in one of the Middle East's ancient civilizations, the Byzantine Empire. I knew you wanted to know that! Serve this with rice and Middle Eastern breads.

TURKISH BROILED

1 pound chicken breasts, boneless, skinless
8 ounces plain low-fat yogurt
1 onion, roughly chopped
5 cloves garlic
1 tablespoon paprika
1 teaspoon ground cumin
1 teaspoon dried oregano
Juice of half a lemon
1 teaspoon spice blend
Freshly ground black pepper

1. In a blender or food processor, combine yogurt, onion, garlic, paprika, cumin, oregano, lemon juice, and spice blend.
2. Puree until smooth; pour into a large bowl or baking dish.
3. Rinse chicken; pat dry and season with spice blend and pepper.
4. Add chicken to yogurt mixture.
5. Cover and marinate 2 hours at room temperature or overnight in refrigerator.
6. Heat broiler.
7. Remove chicken from marinade, shaking off excess, and place on a broiling pan.
8. Broil, 3 to 4 inches from heat, for 6 minutes per side or until crisp on the outside and cooked through.

Serves 4

Calories per serving 185
Cholesterol, mg 69.2
Calories from fat, % 14
Sodium, mg 116

You'll love—Ankara lot—
about this recipe once you've
tried it with couscous.

TURKISH IN LIME JUICE

6 chicken breasts (4–6 ounces each)
3 tablespoons unsalted butter

For the sauce:
  Juice of 2 limes
  ¼ teaspoon cayenne pepper (or to taste)
  3 teaspoons coriander leaves, finely chopped
  1 teaspoon cumin
  1 teaspoon fresh ginger, chopped
  8 small green onions, chopped

1. Place sauce ingredients in an electric blender or food processor. Blend on high until smooth.
2. Pour the sauce over chicken breasts. Marinate and refrigerate for 3 hours, turning 3 or 4 times.
3. Melt the butter in a heavy skillet on high heat. Brown the breasts well on both sides. When brown, pour the marinade over the chicken.
4. Cover the skillet and cook on low heat for 40 minutes or until tender.

Serves 6
Calories per serving 168
Cholesterol, mg 76
Calories from fat, % 30
Sodium, mg 76.1

URUGUAY CHICKEN AND POTATO STEW

A wonderfully warming stew for those cold winter nights—unless you don't experience winter where you live…then just enjoy it for its flavors. Serve this with a rustic bread and a light salad.

3-pound boiled chicken
5 cups chicken stock
1 dried red chili (or more if you have no taste buds left!)
3 each, unpeeled small red and Yukon gold potatoes, cut into 1" pieces
1 each, large sweet potato, Spanish onion, cut into 1" pieces,
8 ounces carrots cut into 1" pieces,
½ teaspoon each ground coriander, pepper, and spice blend
2 to 3 ears corn cut into 4 pieces
⅓ cup low-fat evaporated milk
¼ cup cilantro, minced
1 peeled, sliced avocado (optional)*
1½ tablespoons capers, drained

1. Skin chicken, heat stock and chili over medium high heat.
2. Add potatoes, onions, carrots, coriander, spice blend, and pepper.
3. Bring mixture to boil, cover, and reduce heat to low. Simmer 10 minutes.
4. Add chicken and corn.
5. Continue cooking until vegetables are tender, 8 to 10 minutes.
6. Add evaporated milk and cilantro. Adjust seasonings to taste.
7. Serve in bowls over rice garnished with avocado and capers.

Serves 6

Calories per serving 464
Cholesterol, mg 88.9
Calories from fat, % 29
Sodium, mg 131

*Nutritional information does not include avocado.

UZBEKISTAN

3 pounds chicken breasts, skinless
1 carrot, sliced into 1" pieces
1 stalk celery, sliced into 1" pieces
Spice blend and pepper to taste

For the sauce:
    8 ounces of fresh bing cherries, pitted
    ⅓ cup seedless raisins
    2 teaspoons unsalted butter
    1 teaspoon sugar
    1 cup plus 4 ounces water
    4 teaspoons arrowroot

1. Place chicken, carrot, and celery in a large pot and cover with water. Add spice blend and pepper, bring to a boil, cover, simmer over low heat 45 minutes to an hour, or until fork tender.
2. Remove the chicken and keep warm.
3. Strain the stock, reserving 2 cups.

Sauce:
1. Cook the cherries in a small amount of water over low heat about 15 minutes or until they are soft.
2. Strain the juice and set aside.
3. Rub the cherries through a fine strainer and return to the juice.
4. Add raisins, sugar, and stock to the cherry mixture.
5. Blend the butter and arrowroot with a little of the liquid and add to the cherry sauce.
6. Stir well, bringing sauce to a boil over high heat.
7. Reduce heat to low, simmer 10 minutes, stirring frequently.
8. Spoon sauce over chicken at table.

Serves 6
Calories per serving 303
Cholesterol, mg 135
Calories from fat, % 13
Sodium, mg 172

Another summertime-sounding dinner you can enjoy year around. Serve with squash and a green vegetable. A veritable explosion of color!

VERY BERRY CHICKEN

1 pound chicken breasts, boneless, skinless
1 tablespoon unsalted butter
¼ cup chopped onions
3 tablespoons raspberry jelly
½ cup fresh blackberries
3 tablespoons apple cider vinegar
¼ cup low-fat evaporated milk

1. Cut chicken breasts in half.
2. Sauté in butter in skillet about 5 minutes over medium heat. Turn chicken.
3. Add onion and cook until tender, about 5 minutes more.
4. Remove chicken and keep warm.
5. Add jelly, blackberries, and vinegar to skillet. Scrape pan and stir.
6. Boil 1 minute to slightly reduce liquid.
7. Add evaporated milk and heat.
8. Pour sauce over chicken.

Serves 4
Calories per serving 226
Cholesterol, mg 77.3
Calories from fat, % 22
Sodium, mg 91.8

Note: If you have the room, freeze fresh berries whole to use year-round. You can easily substitute fresh raspberries or thawed frozen berries.

VIETNAMESE CINNAMON GARLIC

4 ounces boneless, skinless chicken breast per serving
1½ teaspoons sesame oil
1 teaspoon cinnamon
1½ teaspoons low-sodium soy sauce
1 teaspoon honey
2 to 3 cloves garlic, pressed

1. Marinate the chicken pieces 1 hour at room temperature.
2. Drain, reserving the marinade for basting.
3. Grill chicken pieces 20–25 minutes over medium coals.

Only beginning to be known and appreciated in American kitchens, Vietnamese cooking is as simple as it is sophisticated. Serve with the ubiquitous bowl of rice.

Sesame

Serves as many as you want!
Calories per serving 149
Cholesterol, mg 65.3
Calories from fat, % 20
Sodium, mg 116

O.K., so I wanted another
recipe to start with a "V"!
Even if you call this one
"winter vegetables," it's
colorful, easy to make, great
tasting, self-contained
and healthy.

VINTER VEGETABLES

3 pounds chicken breasts, skinless
Spice blend and freshly ground black pepper to taste
16 baby carrots (or three large carrots)
16 scallions (green onions)
8 brussels sprouts
1 russet potato
½ pound parsnip
4½ cups chicken broth
1 tablespoon unsalted butter
1 tablespoon flour
1 tablespoon freshly grated horseradish (or to taste)
¼ teaspoon Tabasco sauce
¼ cup fresh parsley, chopped

1. Place the chicken breast halves on a flat surface and trim away and discard fat.
2. Sprinkle the chicken breasts with spice blend.
3. If using large carrots, cut into sticks about 2". long and ½" thick. Trim the root end from the scallions. Cut off most of the green part, leaving pieces about 3" long. Trim the sprouts. If they are large, cut them in half.
4. Peel the potato and cut into ¾" cubes. Put them into a bowl of cold water to prevent discoloration.
5. Peel the parsnip and cut into sticks about 1" long ½" wide.
6. Put 4 cups broth in a large, wide, kettle, and add the carrots, sprouts, drained potato, and parsnip.
7. Sprinkle with spice blend.
8. Bring to a boil and let simmer 5–6 minutes.
9. Add the chicken breasts, in one layer, and the scallions. Cover and cook about 7 minutes.
10. Meanwhile, melt the butter in a saucepan, and add the flour, stirring with a wire whisk.
11. When blended and smooth, add the remaining broth, stirring rapidly with a wire whisk. Add the horseradish and Tabasco sauce.
12. Sprinkle the chicken and vegetables with the parsley.

Serves 6
Calories per serving 351
Cholesterol, mg 137
Calories from fat, % 14
Sodium, mg 176

WINE POACHED

1 pound chicken breasts, skinless, boneless
½ pound fresh mushrooms, sliced
½ teaspoon tarragon
¼ teaspoon freshly ground pepper
2 tablespoons fresh parsley, chopped
¾ cup dry white wine

1. Place chicken and mushrooms in a large skillet.
2. Sprinkle with spice blend, tarragon, pepper, and parsley.
3. Pour wine over chicken.
4. Cover and simmer 30 minutes or until chicken is tender.
5. Serve with sauce remaining in skillet.

There are two basic types of French cooking: "cuisine régionale" and "haute cuisine." This recipe is the first type—the simple cooking of the peasants, spectacular in its simplicity. Serve with crusty bread, wide noodles, a salad and some apple cider. Très magnifique!

Serves 4
Calories per serving 162
Cholesterol, mg 65.7
Calories from fat, % 9
Sodium, mg 77.7

Xeres (now Jerez) is a town near Cadiz in Spain. "X" in Spanish is pronounced like "sh" in English, so you can call this "Sherry-Style". You can call it "Rhonda" if you want, as long as you have a chance to enjoy this "delicioso" meal. Serve it with saffroned rice and a glass of fine Spanish "xeres."

XERES BREASTS

2 large chicken breasts, skinless (about 1½ pounds each), cut into six pieces
2 tablespoons olive oil (Spanish, if possible), divided
⅓ cup sherry wine vinegar
Spice blend to taste
1½ tablespoons low-sodium tomato paste
8 ounces mushrooms
2 tablespoons, parsley, chopped fine

1. Trim excess fat from breasts. Sprinkle with spice blend and set aside.
2. Quarter larger mushrooms and cut smaller ones in half. Set aside.
3. Heat 1 tablespoon oil in a nonreactive pan over high heat and brown chicken.
4. Transfer chicken to a serving plate and pour off any remaining fat.
5. Reduce heat to medium, add vinegar, and dissolve the tomato paste in mixture.
6. Return chicken breasts to pan.
7. Cover and cook 3 minutes. Uncover and cook until chicken is done (5–7 minutes).
8. While chicken is cooking, heat ½ tablespoon of olive oil in a saucepan and cook the mushrooms 4–5 minutes.
9. When serving, arrange chicken and mushrooms on platter.
10. Whisk remaining ½ tablespoon olive oil into pan.
11. Add parsley and juices that collected on serving plate into the sauce.
12. Pour sauce over chicken and mushrooms. Serve immediately.

Serves 6

Calories per serving 211
Cholesterol, mg 82.2
Calories from fat, % 28
Sodium, mg 97.1

YASSA AU POULET DE LA CASAMANCE
(SENEGAL)

2 pounds chicken breasts, skinless, boneless
1 lemon
3 pounds white onions, thinly sliced
½ cup parsley, chopped
1 tablespoon coarse black pepper
1 tablespoon spice blend
3 bay leaves
1 teaspoon thyme
1 teaspoon crushed red pepper (or to taste)
1 cup lemon juice
2 ounces canola oil
1 quart chicken stock
Watercress and parsley for garnish

1. Preheat oven to 375°.
2. Cut lemon in half; rub over chicken breasts.
3. Spread chickens out in a 12" x 18"x 2" baking pan.
4. Cover with onions, parsley, black pepper, spice blend, bay leaves, thyme, and crushed red pepper.
5. Pour lemon juice and oil over the chickens. Allow marinating 30 minutes.
6. Remove the chickens and broil until brown on all sides and are about half done.
7. Simmer the onion mixture over direct heat stirring up from bottom to prevent onions from browning.
8. Cook no longer than 5 minutes.
9. Return chicken to pan, smothering with the onions.
10. Pour 1 quart chicken stock over the mixture.
11. Bake 20 minutes until onions turn a light golden color.
12. Serve with yassa onion mixture on top of rice. Garnish with watercress or parsley.

The influence of French food in Senegal is unmistakable. A "yassa" is a dish that uses a lemon-based marinade. Serve with boiled white rice.

Serves 8
Calories per serving 283
Cholesterol, mg 65.7
Calories from fat, % 29
Sodium, mg 89

From the shadows of Africa's magnificent Victoria Falls comes this surprisingly mild dish. The choice is yours, serve with couscous or over yellow or brown rice.

ZAMBIAN

3 pounds chicken breasts, skinless
2 teaspoons cinnamon
1 teaspoon ground cloves
1 tablespoon canola oil
1 medium chopped onion
1 clove pressed garlic
¾ cup orange juice
3 tablespoons raisins
1 ounce almonds (optional)

1. Season chicken with cinnamon, cloves, spice blend, and pepper.
2. Heat oil over medium heat.
3. Cook chicken till brown, about 10 minutes. Remove.
4. Add onion to pan and cook 3 minutes, until soft. Add garlic, cook another minute. Return chicken to pan, add orange juice and raisins.
5. Cover and simmer 15 minutes
6. Garnish with almonds.

Serves 6
Calories per serving 266
Cholesterol, mg 110
Calories from fat, % 17
Sodium, mg 125

ZUCCHINI TAJINE

2 pounds chicken breasts, skinless, boneless
2 pounds zucchini
3 tablespoons olive oil
2 pounds onions
2 cloves garlic
Spice blend to taste
1 teaspoon freshly ground black pepper
½ teaspoon turmeric
2 cups water

1. Cut zucchini into 2" long pieces. Chop onions and garlic.
2. Heat the oil in a pan, add chicken, onion, garlic, spice blend, pepper, and turmeric. Cook over low heat, 5 minutes.
3. Raise the heat and bring to a boil. Cover the pan, lower heat to simmer, and cook 30 minutes.
4. Add the zucchini and cook 15 minutes. The onion forms a slightly thick sauce that's quite flavorful.

The special dish this is prepared in is called a tajine (ta-hee-na). Zucchini tajine is a specialty of Jews in Morocco. It makes a great company dinner because it's easy to do and looks great. Serve over couscous.

Serves 8

Calories per serving 226
Cholesterol, mg 65.7
Calories from fat, % 28
Sodium, mg 78.8

STORING CHICKEN

	Refrigerated	Frozen
Cooked	1 to 2 days	6 months with solid pieces
Pieces—raw	1 to 2 days	9 months
Whole—raw	1 to 2 days	12 months

SPICES AND HERBS TIMETABLE

The manager of a spice store (and quite a nice man) gave me the following rules for storing and freezing spices and herbs. Here's a timetable for knowing when your spices and herbs have lost their flavor and potency. Always store your spices and dried herbs in a glass bottle with a screw top in a dark, cool area.

Years	Spices
5	mustard (ground), peppercorns (whole)
4	cloves (whole), dill seed, pepper (ground black or cayenne)
3	bay leaves (whole), cinnamon sticks, cumin seeds, curry powder, garlic (minced or powdered), garlic-spice blend
2	basil, chili powder, cloves (ground), coriander, dill weed, ginger, marjoram, nutmeg (ground), onion powder, onion flakes, oregano, paprika (ground), parsley flakes, rosemary (ground),tarragon leaves, thyme
1	cinnamon, ground basil, marjoram, rosemary, thyme

FREEZING FRESH HERBS

Basil
> Blanch sprigs a few seconds in boiling water, then drop them in ice water. Pat sprigs dry and then pack them flat in small plastic bags, removing all air. Seal and freeze.

Chives
> Bunch the spears, then slice fine with a very sharp knife. Freeze the bits loose on a baking sheet. When frozen, pack tightly into a clean, dry, screw-top jar. Cover the jar and place in the freezer.

Cilantro
> Pick the leaves from the stem, then puree in a blender with a little water. Freeze the puree in an ice cube tray. Unmold the cubes, pack in a freezer-weight bag, press out all the air, seal the bag, and store in the freezer.

Dill
> Mince the leaves fine, freeze loose on a baking pan, pack quickly into a clean, dry screw-top jar, and freeze at once.

Tarragon
> Prepare the same way as basil, but freeze the sprigs in a clean, dry, screw-top jar.

Marjoram, Mint, Oregano, Parsley, Rosemary, Sage, Savory, and Thyme
> Blanch, chill, and pack in the same way as Basil.

THE FAT TRUTH
or
What does what?

Monounsaturated (cooking oils)
> Olive oil, canola oil, avocados, nuts
> Lower LDLs
> Neutral on HDLs
> May lower triglycerides

Polyunsaturated (cooking oils)
> Corn, soy, safflower,
> Lower HDLs and LDLs
> May raise triglycerides

Saturated
> Tropical oils, animal fats, meats, dairy products
> Raise HDLs
> Raise LDLs
> Raise triglycerides

Transfatty acids (gives extra body)
> Hydrogenated vegetable oils, margarine
> Raise LDLs slightly
> Lower HDLs slightly

Omega 3
> Fatty fish, fish oil, slax seeds
> Lower LDLs
> May raise HDLs
> Retard clotting
> Relieve inflammation

INDEX OF INGREDIENTS

Courtesy of M.David Leeds

ABOUT THE AUTHOR
(BY THE AUTHOR)

I was born and raised in Mamaroneck, New York. My love for food began with formula and continues to this day!

By the time I graduated from Emerson College with a bachelor's and master's degree in theater, I had worked summers as a "salad man" at a beach club snack bar, and spent some time as a page at NBC and an intern with ABC News. Meanwhile I was perfecting my use of high-calorie, highly-salted and high-cholesterol meals and snacks. But at least my cooking techniques were improving at the same time!

I got married and divorced, and taught high school for two years. Then I spent the next ten years in the exciting field of advertising and public relations. This raised my blood pressure to dangerously high levels, and that's when I had my heart attack.

Undaunted, I continued cooking, eating and working. Sure enough, by July of 1993 I needed a heart transplant. So I went to UCLA where they gave me a new one.

Figuring I'd spent enough time in hospitals, I vowed to change my eating habits and improve my culinary expertise. Thus began the research for this book and a whole new way of life. To my everlasting delight, everything tasted so much better that I decided to share it with the world!

Jeffrey Leeds
Sherman Oaks, California
May, 1999